Color Theory
With Pencils & Mandalas

Dawn Devine & George Goncalves

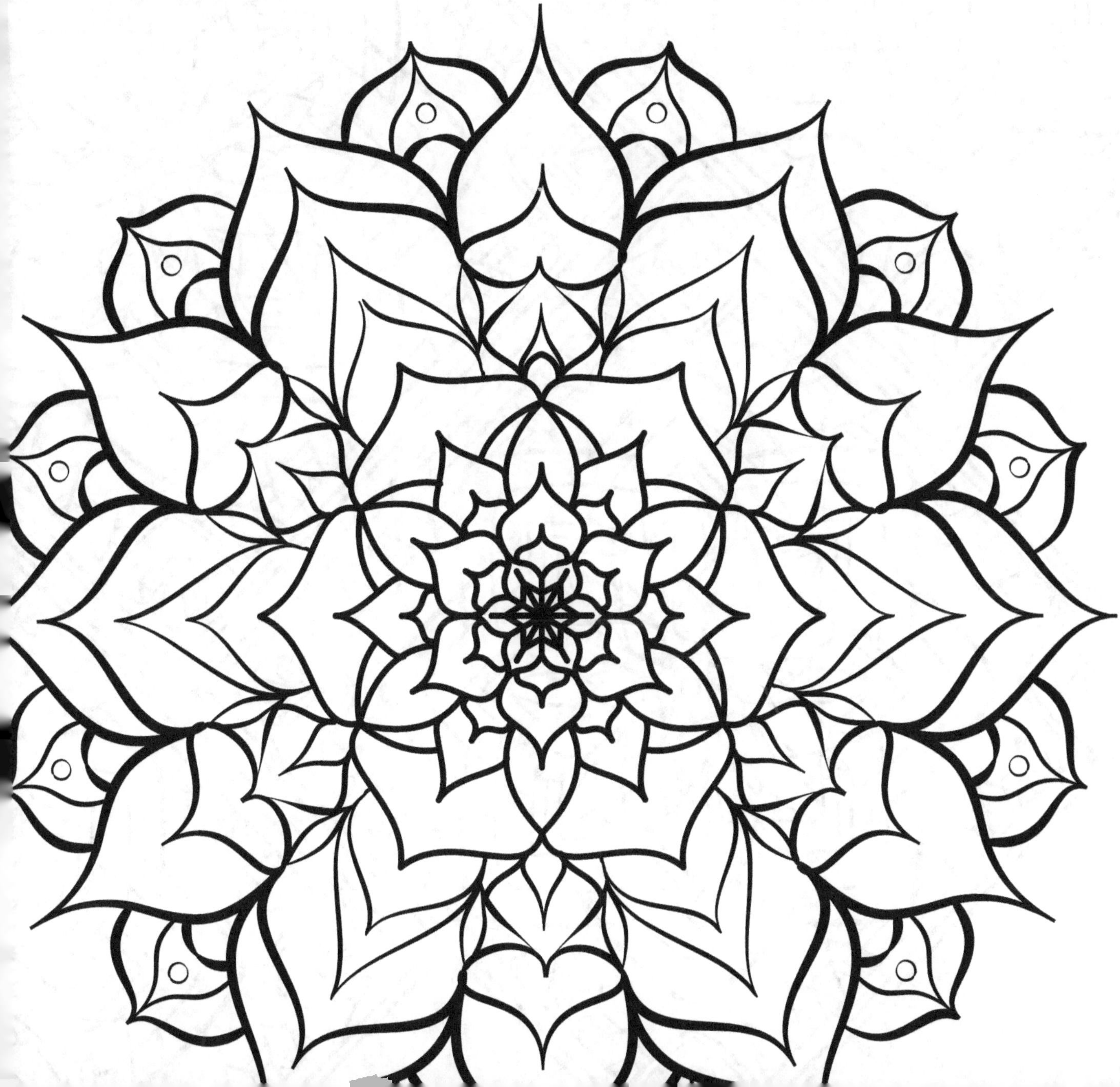

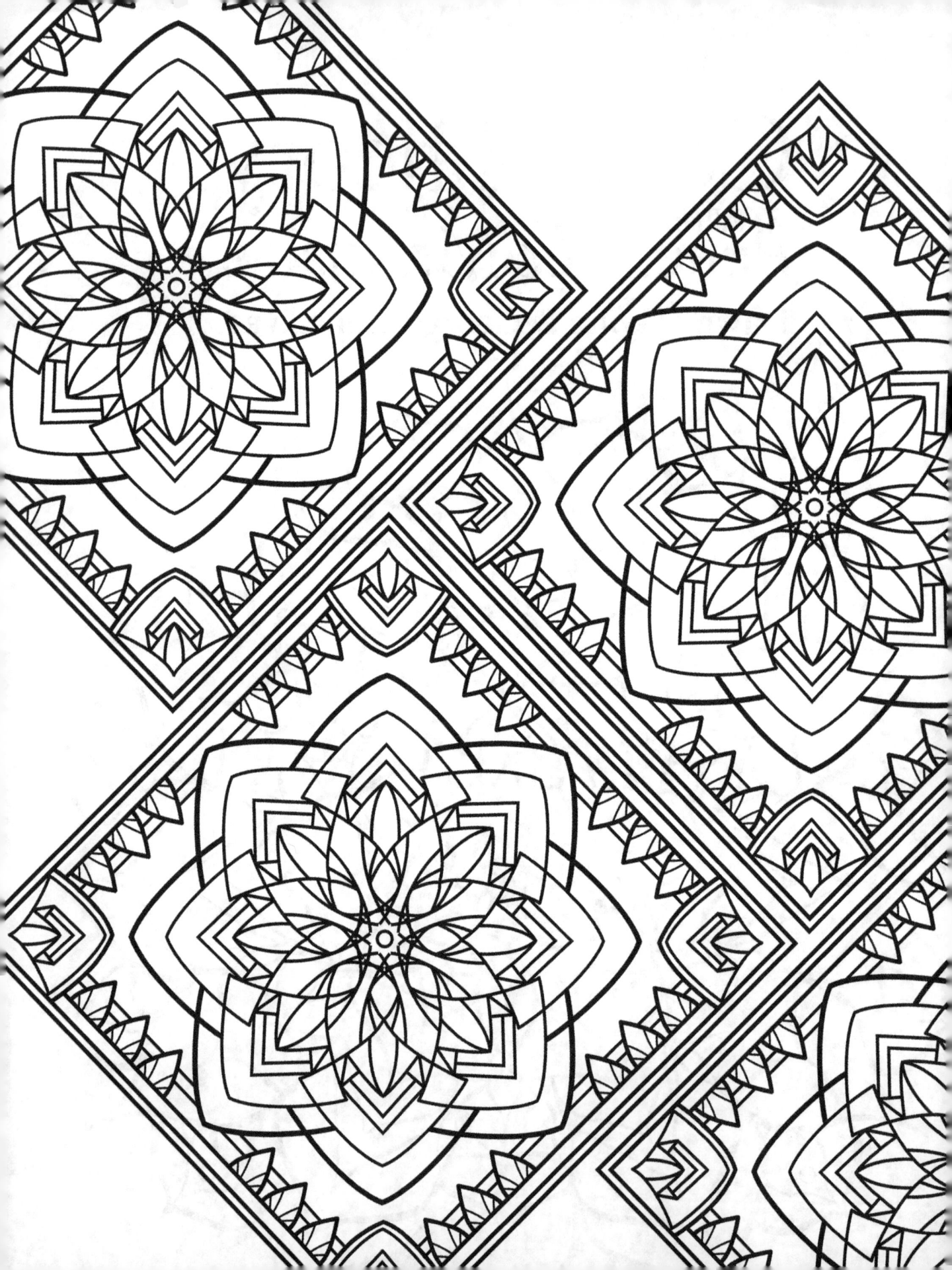

Color Theory
With Pencils & Mandalas

Dawn Devine & George Goncalves

**Think Like
A Designer**

**Workshop
in a Book**

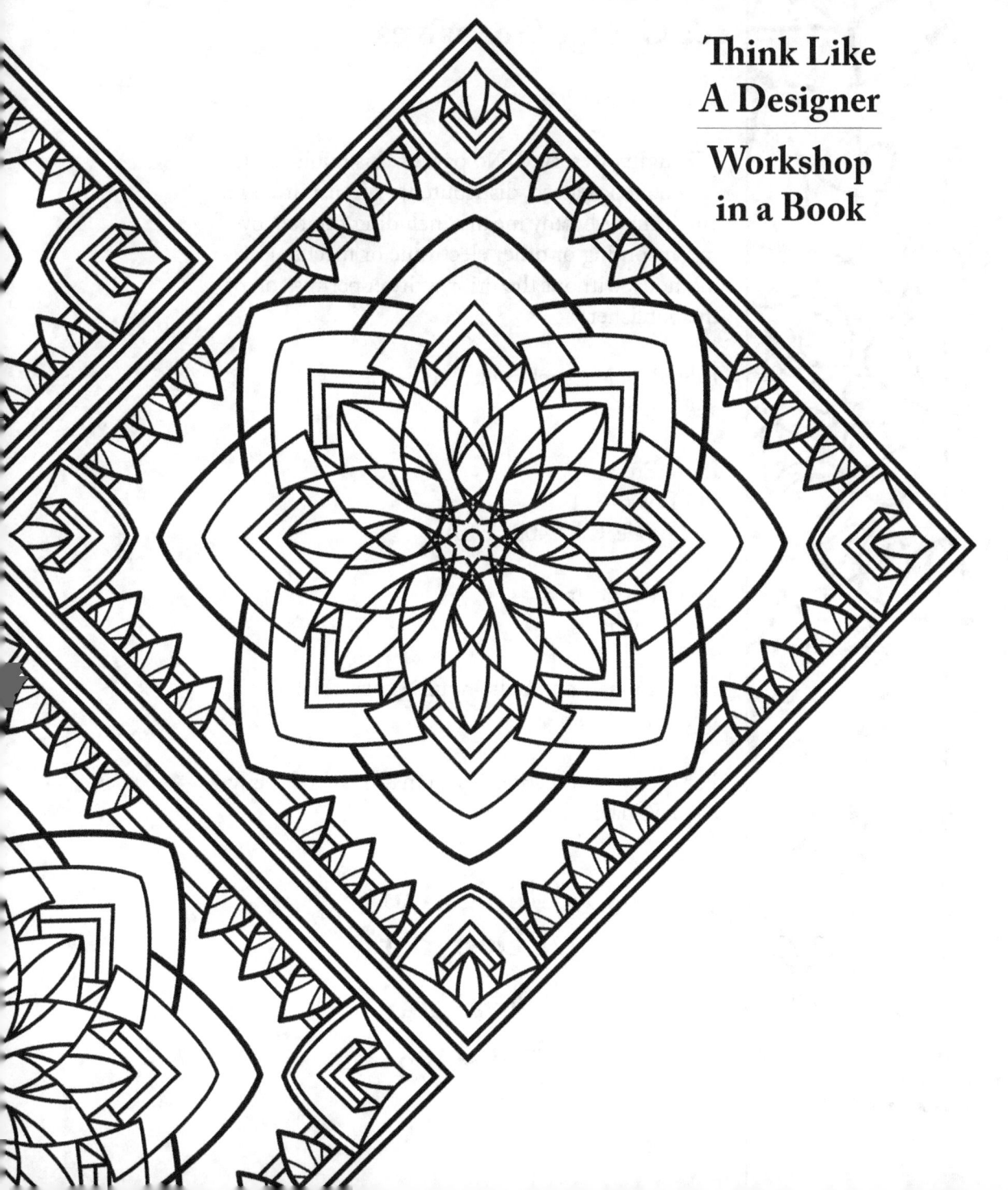

Color Theory
with Pencils & Mandalas
By Dawn Devine
& George Goncalves

Edited by Michael Hyde, Joe Engledow and Jerry Case.

Ibexa Press
PO Box 64391
Sunnyvale, CA 94088 USA

www.ibexa.com
www.davina.us

For wholesale and bulk inquiries please email info@ibexa.com

For qustions and comments email Dawn directly davina@davina.us

**Think Like
A Designer**

**Workshop
in a Book**

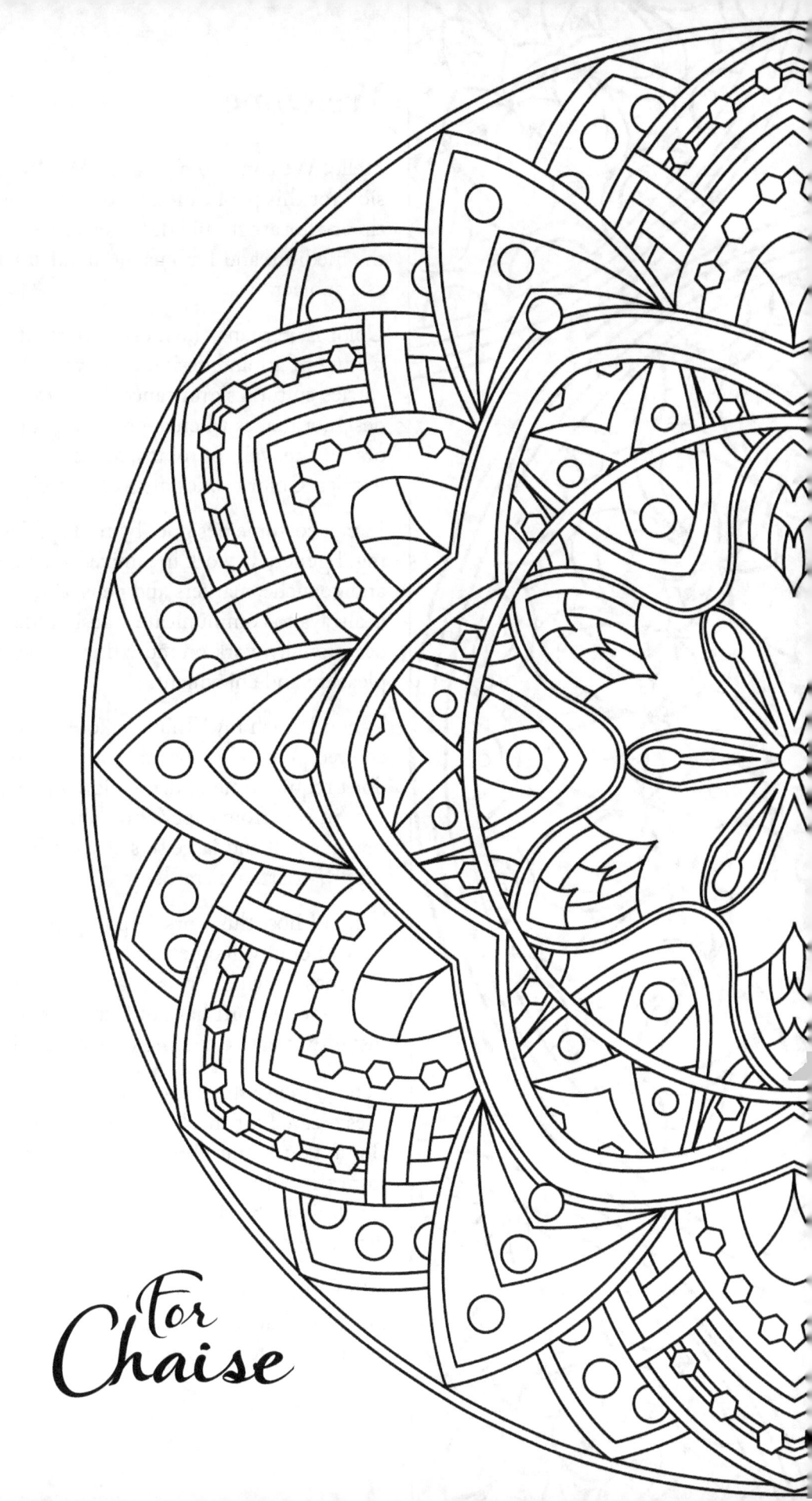

For
Chaise

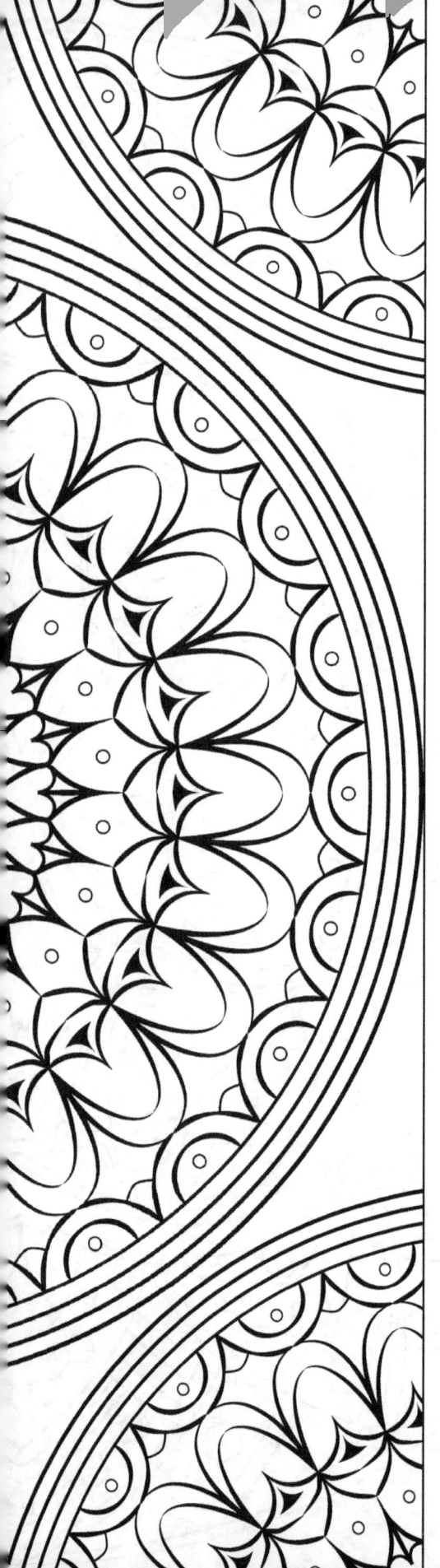

Welcome

Hello! Welcome to my latest "Workshop in a Book." The mission for this publication is to introduce the basic concepts of color theory for artists and designers. I have chosen colored pencils for the medium and I am using mandalas and other geometric forms as a subject.

Color is, perhaps, the most important element of design. It is the feature of art and design that evokes emotion in the viewer and carries cultural significance. It is often the first decision that a designer makes when approaching a project, from choosing colors for the walls of rooms, to selecting the hues for clothing and textiles. Color evokes mood and feeling.

I am a costume designer by trade and a fashion illustrator by training. I generally work in a mixed media mode, using watercolor and goauche, markers and pens, and colored pencils. My mission is always to communicate a design idea in my work, but I will occasionally work on more fine art pieces, but always for my own pleasure and enjoyment.

When I teach my "Think Like A Designer Classes," I choose colored pencils because they are easy to use, not very messy, and don't require time to dry. Colored pencils are widely available and vary in cost from super affordable to fine artist grades. Find pencil sets in small and large sets at your favorite discount, big-box, office supply, or art and craft store.

When I host this workshop in person, my handout includes a variety of empty geometric shapes to experiment with different color schemes. Having forms, shapes, and designs to color with pencil, my students don't have to face the stress of having to draw, and be instantly creative coming up with a subject.

I chose to use the term "mandala" because the bulk of the images created for this book are circular floral and geometric motifs. But as you thumb through the designs, you will see that I pulled from the entire world of design. I've included my thoughts behind the designs that I was inspired by, and suggestions for your own design research.

While this isn't a heavy-hitting deep dive into color theory, it is my hope that you enjoy this instructional coloring book and that it inspires you to get creative!

Dawn Devine aka Davina

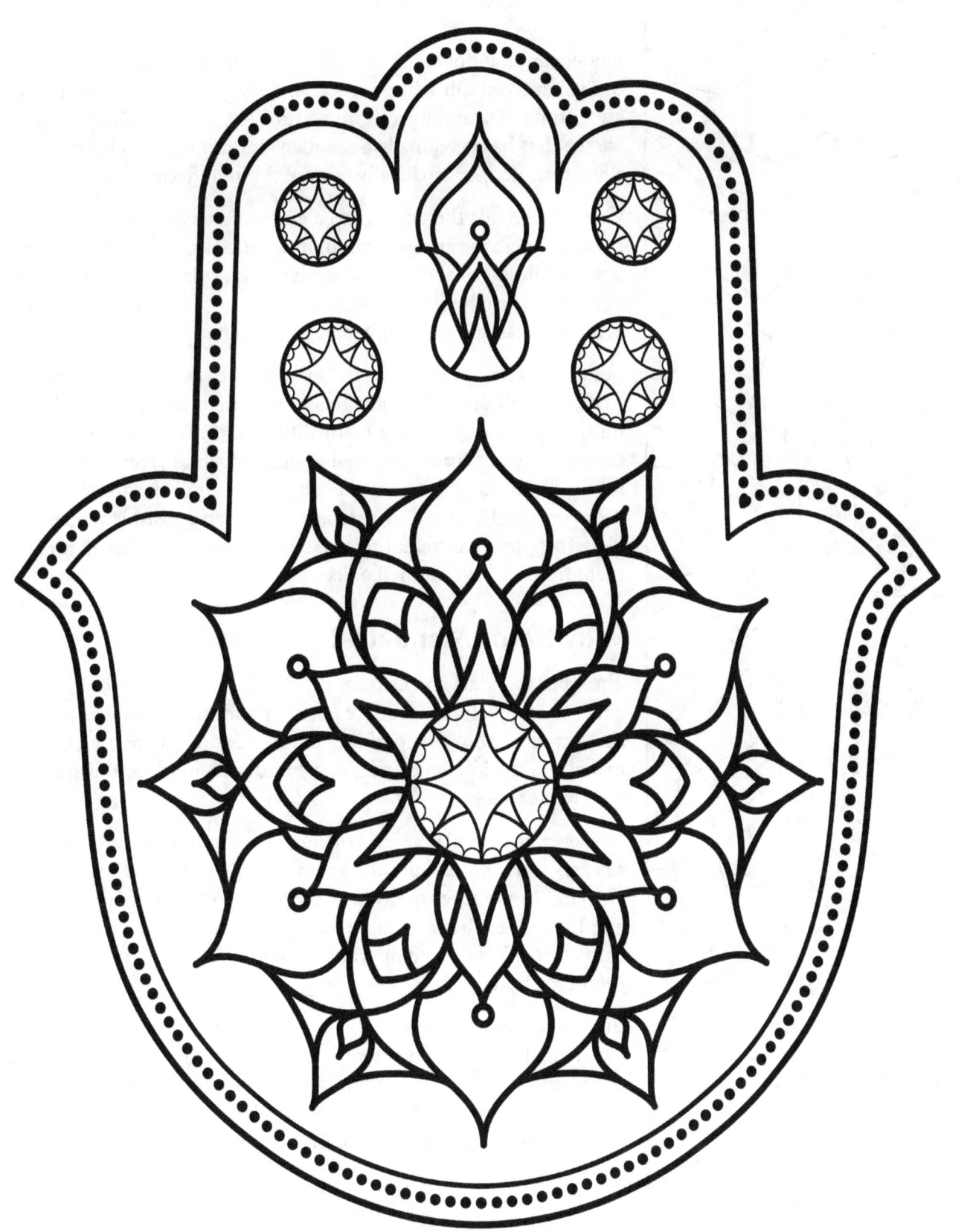

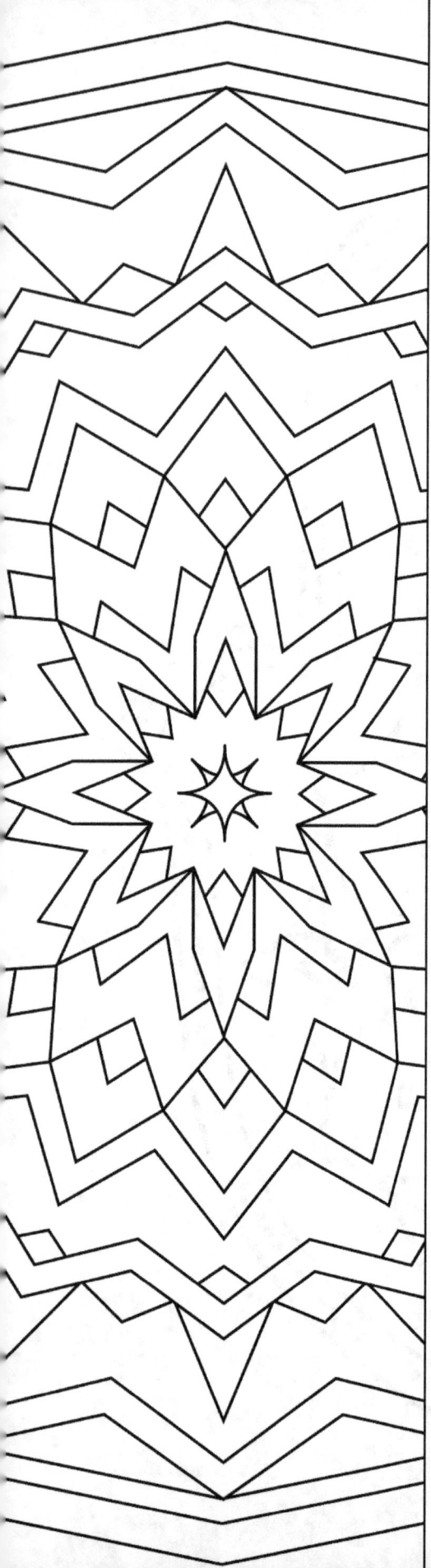

Color and Design

Understanding how different colors interact and relate harmoniously helps you think like a designer. Design is a process that takes an abstract idea and turns it into a finished product. Everything we see that has been made by humans for humans has been designed, crafted, or artistically created through design.

Color is perhaps the one design element that every designer, artist, and craftsperson can agree upon. It has social and cultural impact sending messages about mood of the piece. It is one of the key items in the elements of design, a collection of features of virtually every art, craft, or really, any man-made items.

For a new artist or designer, the mission is to establish a workflow that creatively and efficiently gets from the starting point to the finished product. There are many different kinds of designers in the world today, from industrial design to fashion, architecture to robots. In the arts, there are fine artists and applied artists, 2-dimensional and 3-dimensional, realistic and abstract media. Craftspeople use different media, but still have a process that takes them from idea to finished object.

Why Color Mandalas?

The word mandala comes from the Sanskrit word that means circle or completion. These are geometric form that represent an abstract or symbolic map of the universe. Mandala are used by two of the world's major religions, Hinduism and Buddhism as a meditative tool.

However, the circular geometric motifs are found within design cultures worldwide. From the geometric tile work of the ancient Romans, to the rose windows of the great gothic churches of the middle ages, to the contemporary "Dutch" hex designs found on barns throughout contemporary US, our visual world is filled with geometric patterns.

But no matter what you may call a particular design, their complexity make them a great tool for experimenting with color combinations. Use them to find the color harmonies that appeal to your inner designer. Think about which hues reflect your taste and style and how you will incorporate color into your future designs.

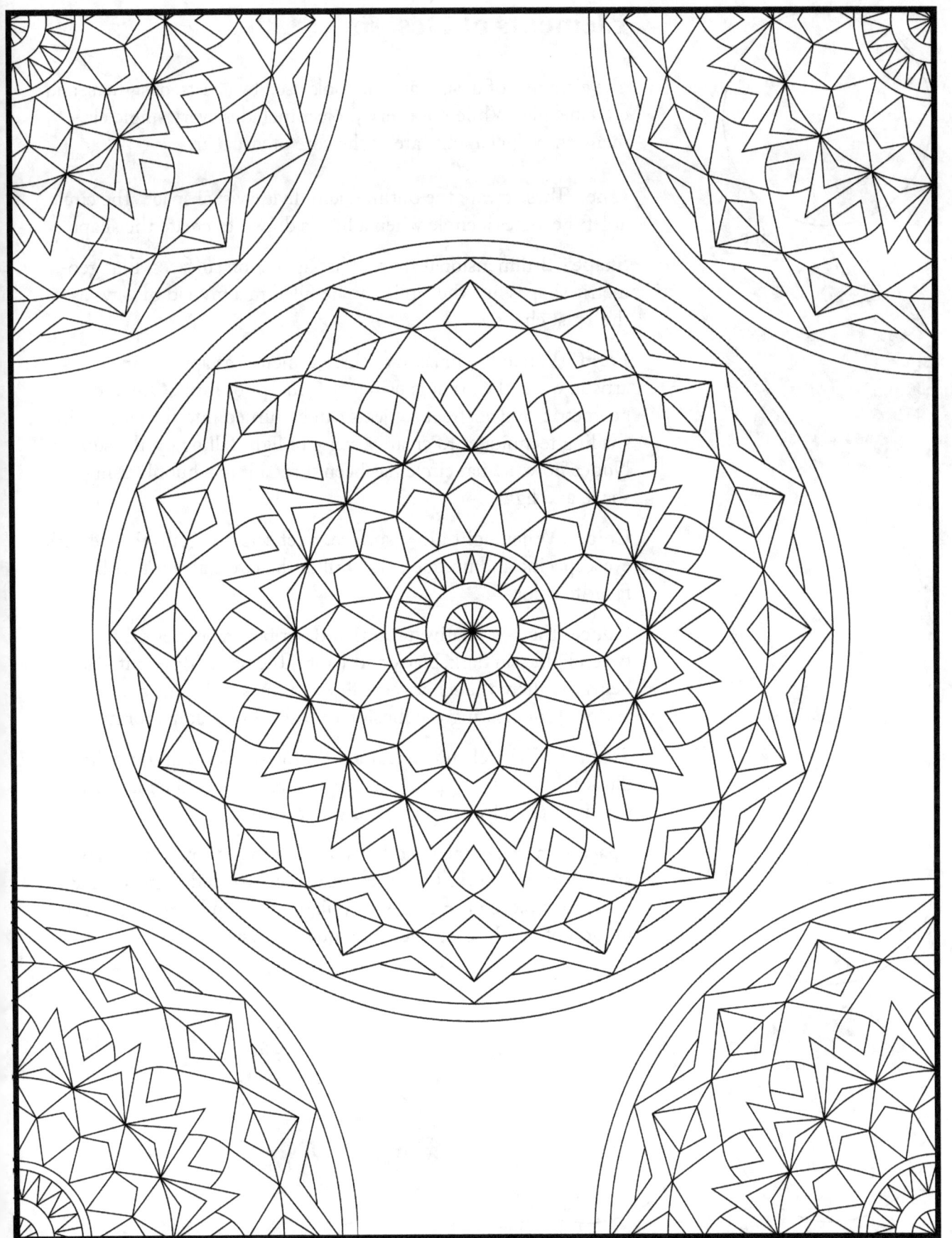

Elements of Design

The elements of design are the tools used by artists, designers, and craftspeople. While not every project includes every single element, these 7 elements are at the core of visual arts.

Line - These create the outlines and divide visual space. The circle at left becomes a circle when a line is drawn to create the shape.

Shape - 2-dimensional shapes that appear on surfaces. Flat geometric shapes like the circle can be filled in a myriad of ways as the artist chooses.

Form - When the illusion of three dimensions appears in an artistic work, the artist is using the concept of form. Organic, geometric, and abstract subjects can be turned into forms by using shading techniques to create a sense of light falling on the subject. Notice how the flat circle has been turned into a bubble using shade and light.

Color - When light hits a surface, it reflects back into the viewer's eye a specific and unique color. Fill in the circle at right with your favorite color.

Value - This is a relative term that describes the relationship between light and dark, black and white. The use of different values helps to differentiate between different lines and shapes, and is essential for creating the illusion of three dimensional forms.

Texture - The feel and appearance of the surface that gives the illusion of a tactile experience. In the circle below, the idea of wetness is implied by the texture of water droplets.

Space - These are the area that surround the various lines, shapes, and forms in a work. These can create positive and negative shapes that give a piece meaning. Manipulating line and form creates the illusion of depth using the technique of perspective.

Line

Shape

Form

Color

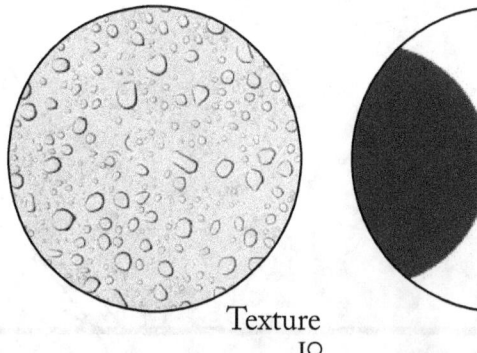

Value

Texture

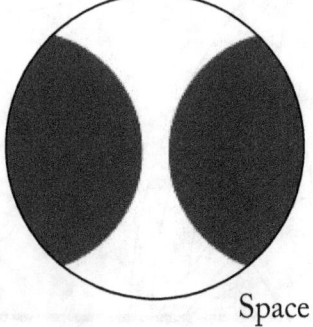

Space

Principles of Design

The principles of design are simply a way of organizing design ideas into topics. Entire books have been devoted to these principles and each designer has their own way of articulating these principles. Here are some brief definitions and examples to get you started. If this topic interests you, we've included several of our favorite design books on page 84.

Pattern - The arrangement and organization of regular repeated elements like shapes, colors, lines, or motifs.

Contrast - A juxtaposition of different design elements to create and accentuate difference.

Emphasis - Accentuating an important element or feature to create a focal point.

Alignment - Arrangement of the parts into a cohesive whole by forming lines, shapes and forms.

Movement - Creating a pathway for the viewer's eye to travel through your piece through your work leading to focal points.

Proportion - The scaling of objects in relation to each other. This includes the relationships between individual parts, but also the relationship between all parts and the whole.

Balance - The distribution of visual weight to create the impression of equal importance.

Unity/Harmony - A harmonious arrangement of design elements. This gives the viewer the sense that all the parts and pieces create a coherent whole.

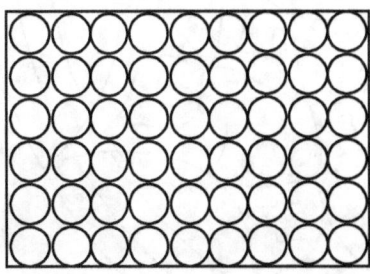

Pattern

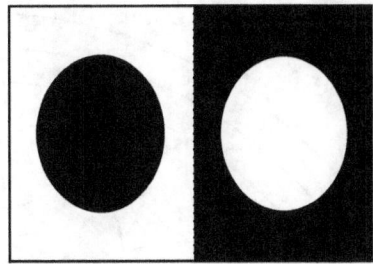

Contrast

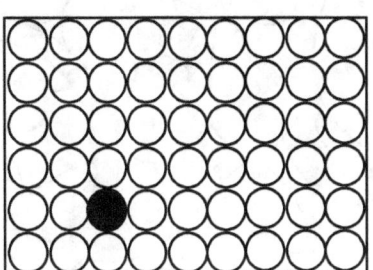

Emphasis

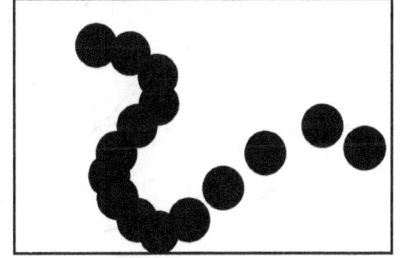

Movement

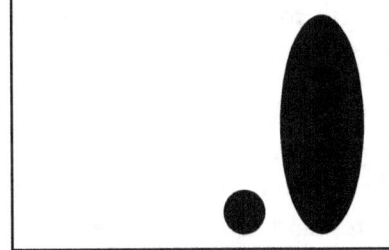

Proportion

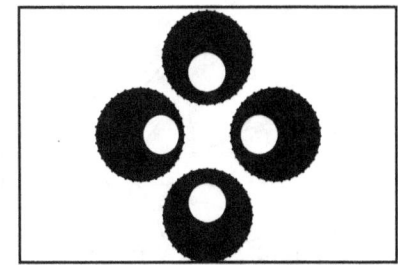

Balance

Unity

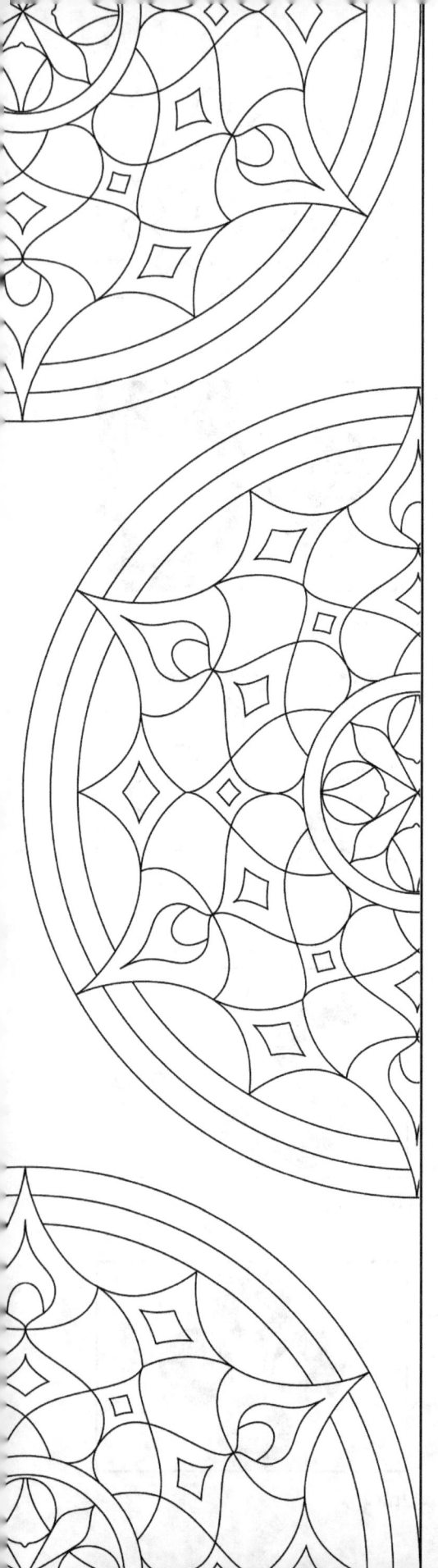

The Color Wheel

The ancestor of our color wheel was invented by none other than the great scientist and thinker Sir. Isaac Newton who discovered that he could break clear light into a rainbow. His experiments in optics lead to his arranging the colors into circular form that is the ancestor to our modern color wheel. Later, the names of his colors were converted into the common mnemonic Roy G. Biv; a false name composed first letters of the rainbow color names: red, orange, yellow, green, blue, indigo, violet.

Over time, the modern color wheel settled on 12 colors which shows the relationships between the three primary, three secondary, and six tertiary colors. On the page opposite is a color wheel ready for you to fill. While it's theoretically possible to create a full 12 shade color wheel just using the three primary colors, red, yellow and blue, most 24 pencil sets include their version of the color wheel basics. Note that not all pencils will have names that match, so as you make swatches of your pencils, notate which colors work for building your color wheel. (For more about pencil swatching, visit page 22.)

While you are filling in your color wheel, use the the inner triangle to practice different levels of pressure between the dotted lines, moving from lightest pressure to create a tint, medium pressure in the center band, and full pressure and intensity in the third section.

Use the large triangles that point to the secondary colors of green, violet and orange to practice building gradients that blend together the colors on around that quadrant of the wheel. Fill in bands of color and try blending the bands together. Alternatively, you can try using just three colors, the two primaries and the secondary to create a smooth even blend.

If you are concerned about selecting your colors, you can simply find a color wheel on line to use as a reference. If you plan on working on more design projects, you might want to invest in a ready-made color wheel to use as a reference from an art or craft supply store. Look for a color wheel with rotating components that will help you identify different color groupings and offers tints, tones and shades.

If your pencil set includes grays and browns, put them in the boxes arrangeing them from lightest and brightest to deep and dark. As you color, use a light pressure on the top and more pressure on the bottom to achive full saturation.

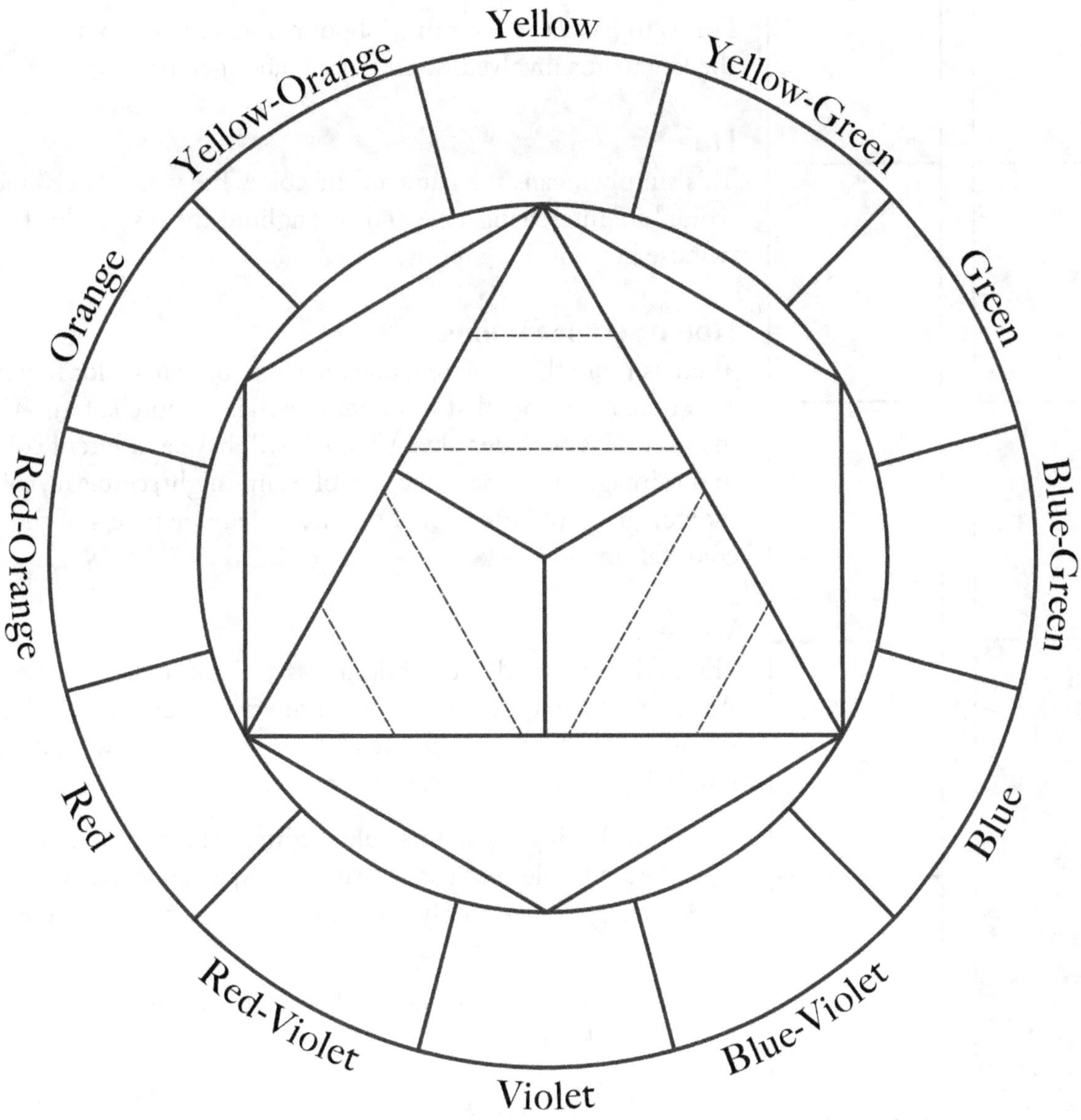

Yellow

Yellow-Orange

Yellow-Green

Orange

Green

Red-Orange

Blue-Green

Red

Blue

Red-Violet

Blue-Violet

Violet

Neutral colors including Greys and Browns

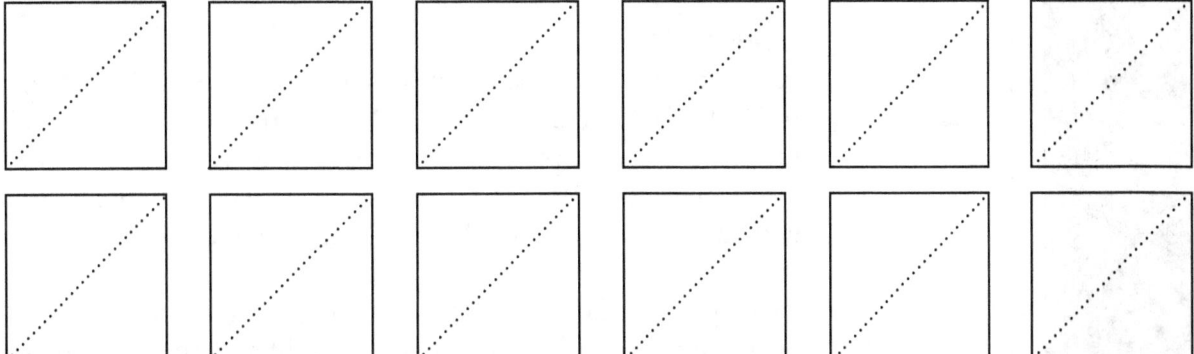

The Language of Color

For us to have a conversation about color, we need to understand the key words involved when talking about color.

Hue

This simply means the name of the color. The words "hue" and "color" are interchangeable and throughout the rest of this book I will use both of these terms.

Hue or color families

There is more than one red, one blue, one brown. Color families are groups of colors that fit under one main umbrella term. For instance, let's consider blue. We each will have a different color in our imagination. Sea blue, sky blue, midnight, cerulean, cobalt, indigo, are all variations on a theme, and are members of the blue color family.

Value

This is the relative degree of lightness and darkness of a color. As an artist and designer, you will not want to use every color in it's most pure form. To achieve different values, you will add the modifying colors of white, grey, and black.

> **Tint:** Adding white to a color lightens the hue, making a less saturated, pale, and pastel. Alternately, when working with pencils, you can simply use less pressure to achieve the same goal.

> **Shade:** Adding black or another, darker color to deepen and darken the hue.

> **Tone:** Adding grey reduces the intensity of the original hue, while still creating a lighter or darker variation of the color. Some designers choose to use shades of brown instead, creating muted tones that some designers refer to as "Mutes."

Gray scale

A gray scale is composed of shades of gray between 100% white to 100% black. In photography, a 10 part gray scale assigns a value to each color; with pure black having a value of 1 and pure white having a value of 10. In art, the gray scale might be more fluid with any number of "steps" between white and black.

Using your blackest pencil, try matching the gray scale to the left by modulating your pressure to create light and mid-tones of gray.

Primary color

There are three primary colors, red, blue and yellow. These are the basic building blocks of color that are blended with other hues, and shades of white grey and black to create an infinite possibility of color.

On the wheel to the right, fill in the yellow, blue and red wedges of this color wheel. Try to make the innermost portions of the wedge lighter by using less pressure. In the middle of the wedge, use more pressure to get the most saturated color. Add black to the outer edge to tone the color.

Secondary colors

These are the basic blends of two primary colors. Yellow and red create orange. Green is made mixing yellow and blue, while purple is a combination of red and blue.

On the wheel at the right, color in the tertiary hues of orange, green and violet. As you color them, vary your pressure to get a tint in the center of the circle, saturated color in the middle of the wedge, and add black to create a shade at the outer edge of the wheel.

Tertiary colors

These are the hues located between the primary and secondary colors on a traditional 12 color wheel. There are six tertiary colors. Try coloring them in on the wheel at right, dividing each wedge into sections to create a tint, a saturated hue, and a shade on the outer edge.

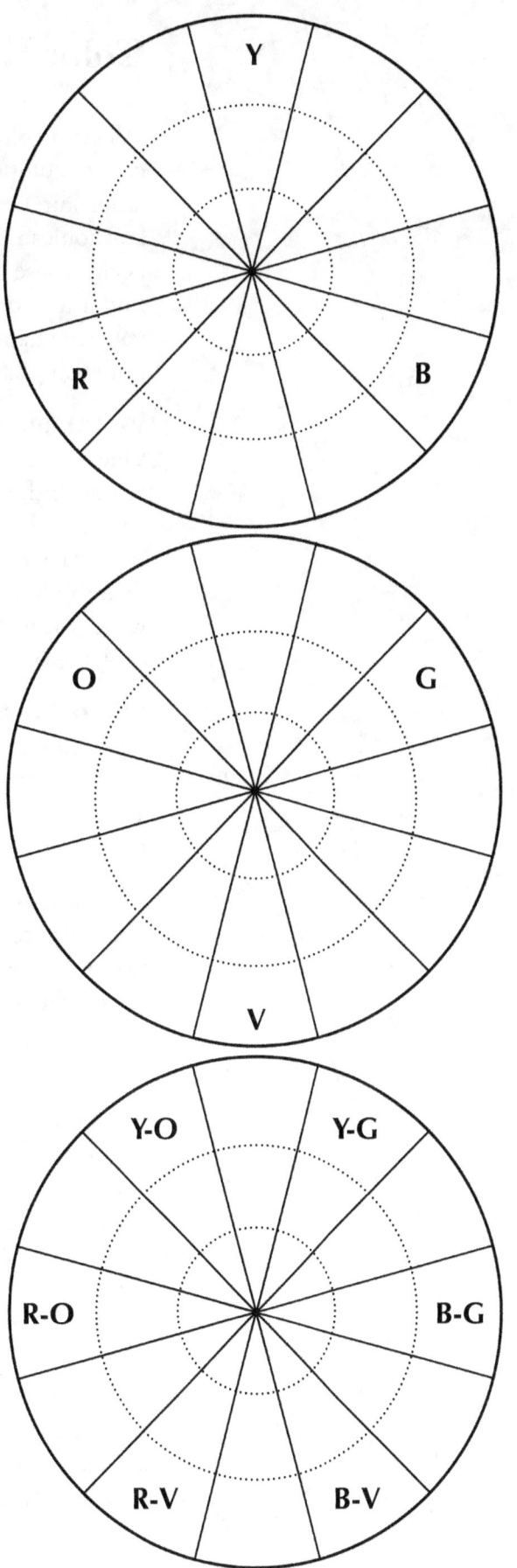

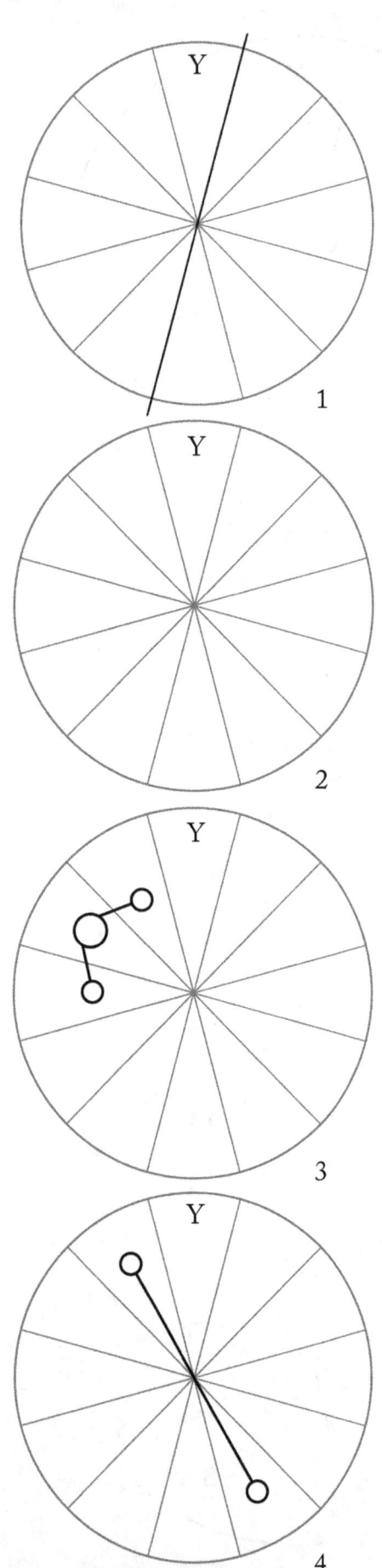

Color Harmonies

Where a color wheel comes in handy is as a tool to efficiently choose color schemes. The colors on the wheel illustrate the relationship between colors. There are some well established color harmonies that successful designers and artists use over and over again. These colors coordinate in ways that people instinctively find interesting. As you look at these relationships, consider how you can change the tones of the colors, making them more pastel or deeply shaded to vary how these color combos look together.

Warm and Cool Colors

One of the easiest ways to break the color wheel into groups is to divide the color wheel between warm and cool colors. Warm colors are brighter, draw the eye and give the illusion of pushing forward, while cool colors tend to give the illusion of receding. The dividing line is between Yellow and Yellow-Green across the color wheel to the line between Red-Violet and Violet. The blue side is cool, the orange side is warm.

Monochromatic Color Scheme

This color scheme is made of only one color. Imagine a black and white photograph, which uses different shades of grey to construct an entire image. If you pick a single color, modulate your values to create contrast.

Analogous Colors

This color scheme is created by choosing a color and using it and two of it's neighbors on the color wheel. Analogous color schemes are soothing and serene like looking at the sea and sky, or the myriad of greens in a forest canopy.

Complementary Colors

The color scheme that creates the most high-contrast are pairing colors directly opposite on the color wheel. These complementary colors are used at full saturation for commercial uses like sports team colors and corporate logos. For greater variety, designers choose to manipulate the colors by desaturating one or both colors.

---

1 - **Warm and Cool colors**
2 - **Monochromatic Colors**
3 - **Analogous colors**
4 - **Complementary colors**

5 - **Split complimentary colors**
6 - **Triadic colors**
7 - **Tetradic colors**
8 - **Square color scheme**

Split Complementary Colors

This color scheme is similar to the complementary, but has three colors. Choosing a color, and then the two colors on each side of its complement. An example is Yellow with red-violet and Blue-violet.

Triadic Colors

For this color scheme, designers use three colors equally spaced on the color wheel. The primary colors form a triadic color scheme.

Tetradic Colors

The tetrad is composed of two pairs of complements. It is easily visualized as a rectangle placed on the color wheel. For example, the colors red and green, blue and orange form a tetrad.

Square Color Scheme

This is a four-color scheme that is also composed of two pairs of compliments. But in the square scheme, the colors are selected by placing a sqaure on your colorwheel. These color schemes often work best when one color is chosen to be dominant or the focal color. An example of a square color scheme is Red and green

Coloring the color harmonies

The coloring harmonies or color schemes are not rules set in stone, but rather, are guidelines for helping you select your color palette. On these two pages, we've created a simple color wheel that you can use as a tool to help you remember these different color schemes. Remember, that though I've marked some of the patterns on these color wheels, you can choose your favorite colors to fill in.

Use Black or the Complementary Color to Deepen a Hue

As you color, try to create smooth gradients or transitions from pale or lightest value of each color at the center, through a pure saturated tone in the middle, and a deeper darker value on the outside edge. You can create this darker tone by adding black, or, as many artists prefer, by adding a hint of the contrasting color. So to deepen the color green, you might choose to add a bit of red, instead of black.

For examples of these color harmonies, see the back cover.

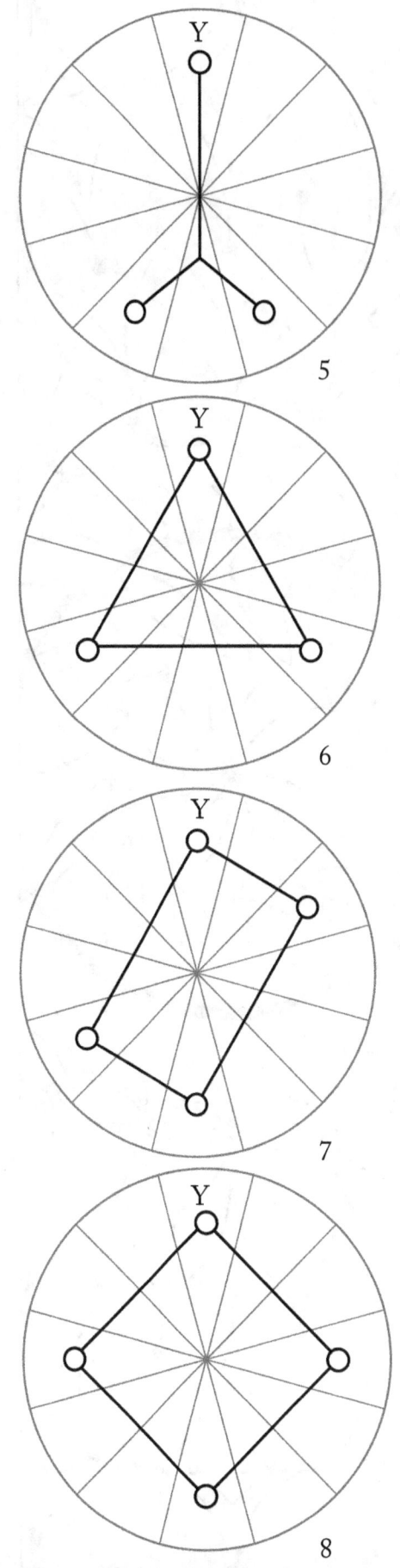

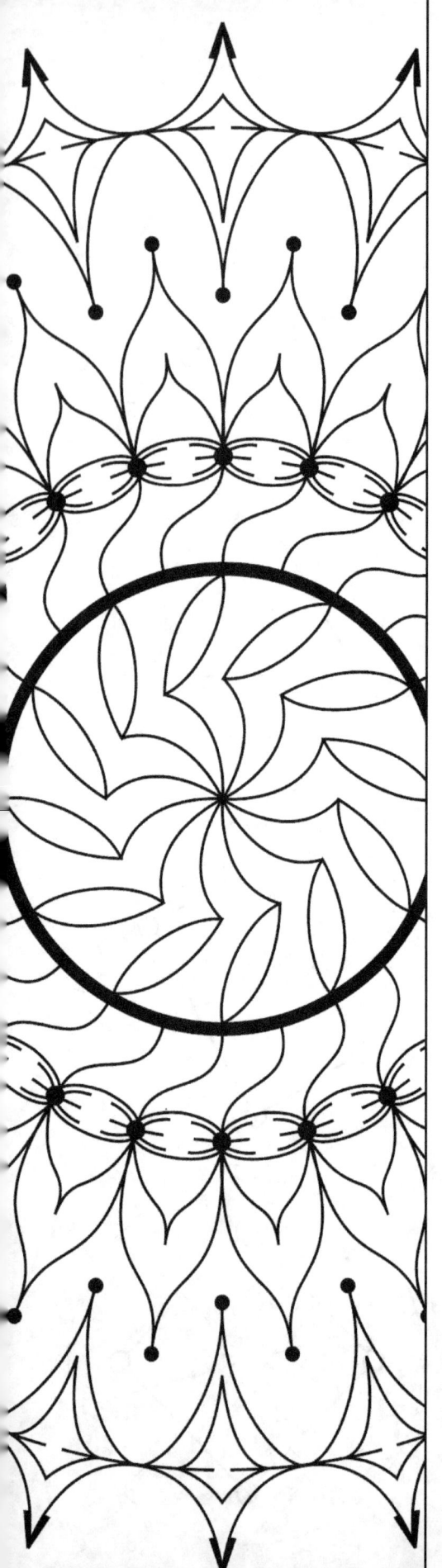

Think Like A Designer

The process of design happens in a wide variety of creative fields from fine arts and crafts, to industrial and packaging design even architecture. Everything you touch and use that is made by people for people has undergone a design process. Some people intuitively know what steps to take when planning a creative project. But for the rest of us, it's a good idea to have a clear idea of the necessary steps for creating a successful design.

Define the Project

The first step is to identify your problem. Are you making a painting? Creating a new can opener? Designing a calendar? The goal here is create a "design brief" that describes what you are creating, how, and for whom. The brief will map out basic criteria like size, shape, use, form and most importantly, the budget for tools, materials, and supplies. Even if you're just working on a personal project at home, it's nice to define your project.

Collect Information

Once your initial ideas mapped out, the next step is to conduct visual research. In general, there are two types of information that designers seek out when they are embarking on a new project.

Look at similar items

For example, if you are designing a chair, you will want to look at other completed chairs by designers you admire, that are in style and in stores today, or pictures of vintage or antique chairs from the past. If you design chairs frequently, you will collect and store your own personal visual library for future chair projects.

Find abstract but apealing images

Look at photographs that appeal to you because of their colors, textures, subject mater, and practically anything that moves you. For instance, you've planned the line and shape of your chair, but you might pull a series of beautiful sunset images to use as inspiration for yellow and orange ombre colored fabric.

Once you have collected a selection of inspirational images, put them together into an inspiration or mood board to reference while you are working on you project. When working with customers, professional designers will use the mood board as a tool for sharing their ideas with their clients. Traditionally, artists, designers and craftspeople have used collage techniques to pin images onto the walls above their workspaces to easily reference. Today, there are many digital options for collecting images together to store on your computer or in the cloud.

Brainstorm & Experiment

Sketch and doodle, collage and paste, or sew and sculpt. No matter what your preferred experimental media is, make small-scale samples to test your ideas, concepts, and theories. As a fashion designer, I do lots of preparatory sketches until I have a clear idea about my design. This includes making color swatches on paper, and then shopping at fabric stores in my area to find colors to match, harmonize, and coordinate.

Make your Plan of Action

When you have a clear idea of where you are headed, begin work on your project. If you are a fine artist, designer, or craftsperson working for yourself, this is where you will make your two key lists; what you need to buy, and what you need to do. For instance, when making garments, I always make a to do list. This way, I won't leave out a vital step, or make extra work by putting things together in a less efficient manner.

Make Samples and Get Feedback

If you are working for a customer or client, you want to make samples, mock-ups, final sketches, or scale models for them to approve of the design, materials, and perhaps most importantly, the budget. Most designers working on projects for others are prepared to bounce between step 4 and 5 until all the questions are answered and a plan is hammered out in the form of a contract.

Create the Finished Product

The best part of the project is making it happen. It's that final moment when you have moved past all the theoretical, conceptual, and abstract ideas, and have created your artwork, design piece, garment, building, or anything at all.

Document the Project

After you have finished creating your work, take the time to document your work. Take photographs throughout the project and of the final piece for your own personal archive and for your public portfolio. While you may not need to maintain a formal portfolio, it's nice to have a record of projects to look back on.

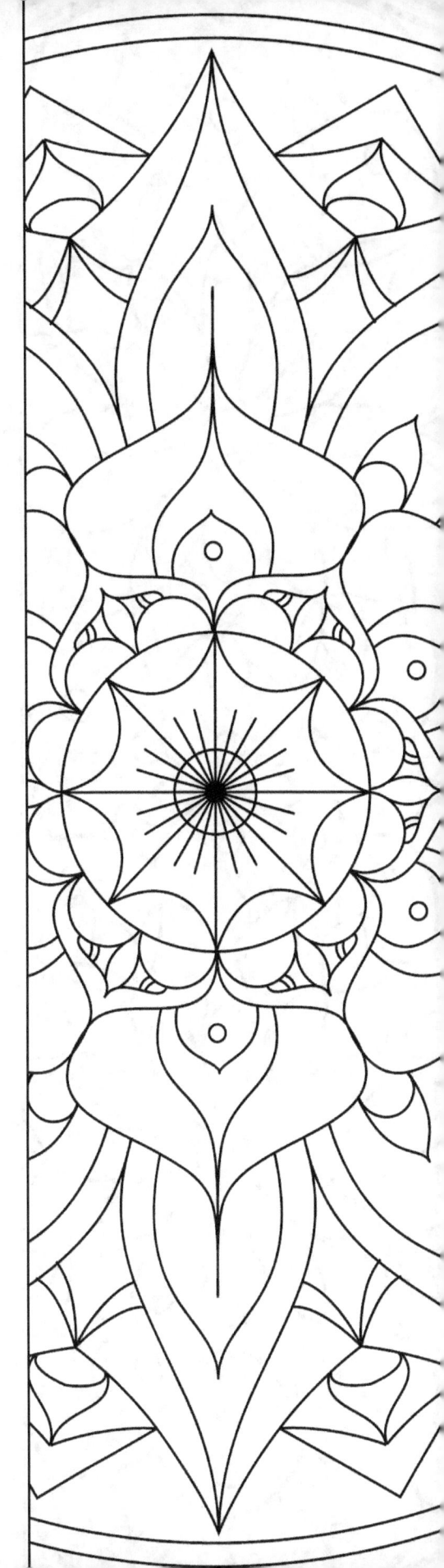

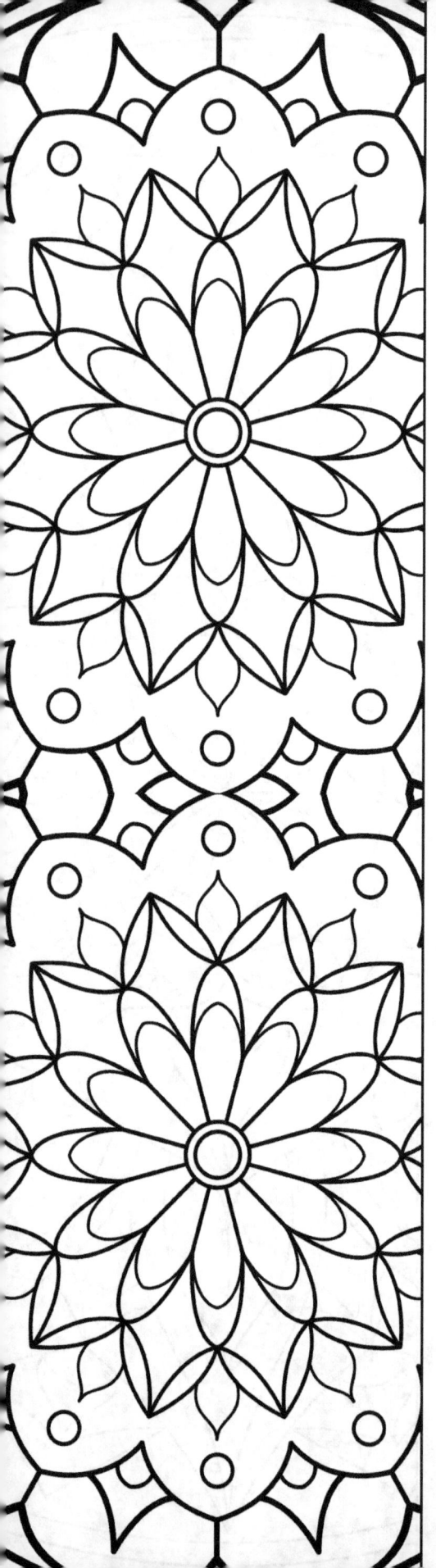

Coloring: Materials and Supplies

When I teach this material in person, I have a course list filled with the tools and supplies needed to complete the class. I've broken this list down into two groups. The first part is a short list of essentials. The second part includes items that enhance the experience of coloring.

Buy the best quality you can afford. Set a budget and do some research. Start with affordable materials, and then as you grow in skill, upgrade. You do not need top-of-the-line artist grade color pencils to color.

Buy what you need to achieve your design goals. For instance, if you want a finely blended look, invest in blending tools.

Use the tools and supplies you buy. Many new artists, designers, and craftspeople fall in love with their supplies and never use them. Don't be afraid to use your art and craft supplies!

Essential Supplies

Set of 12 or 24 colored pencils
It is theoretically possible to draw a complete color wheel with five pencils; red, yellow, blue, black and white. But when you are focused on experimenting with color harmonies, it's nice to have a full color wheel to practice different color combinations without having to blend all your colors.

Pencil Sharpener
A simple hand turned pencil sharpener is required to keep your pencils in good condition. Affordable and easy to find, you might already have one in your collection.

Erasers
There are two different types of erasers that are essential to have on hand. Some artists prefer a firm white vinyl eraser while others prefer kneaded rubber. I find that I use both and keep both handy when working on pieces.

Optional Supplies

Color Wheel
There are many different color wheels available in digital form across internet. However, if you are a working designer, having a physical color wheel with rotating rings can be very helpful if you are choosing colors

Blending Stump or Tortillion
If you like to have a super smooth and blended surface, you can use a tortillion. This is a great way to get smooth blends without adding more color.

Clear or Colorless Blender Pencil
A colorless pencil to assist with clear smooth color blends and create a beautiful finish.

Sand Paper
To help keep your pencils nice and sharp having a handy bit of sandpaper nearby, will allow you to quickly make a sharp tip.

Eraser Shield
These handy little metal or plastic tools allow the artist to erase a specific shape, line or area without worry about slipping.

Black Fine-liner Pen
If you want to "reclaim" lost coloring book lines or if you plan on adding your own lines or doodles to a coloring page, a black-fine-liner pen will allow you to easily draw over your colored pencil. They are available in different line-weights, individually and in sets.

White Gel Pen
If you want to add pure white highlights to your colored drawing, a gel pen allows you to go right over the top without blending into the pencil.

Pencil Pouch or Pen Roll
If your pencil set didn't come in a sturdy container, invest in a dedicated pouch or pencil roll.

Electric Eraser
These do a better job than a traditional hand-held eraser. Electric erasers have a finer tip, which allows you to get into tighter controlled areas.

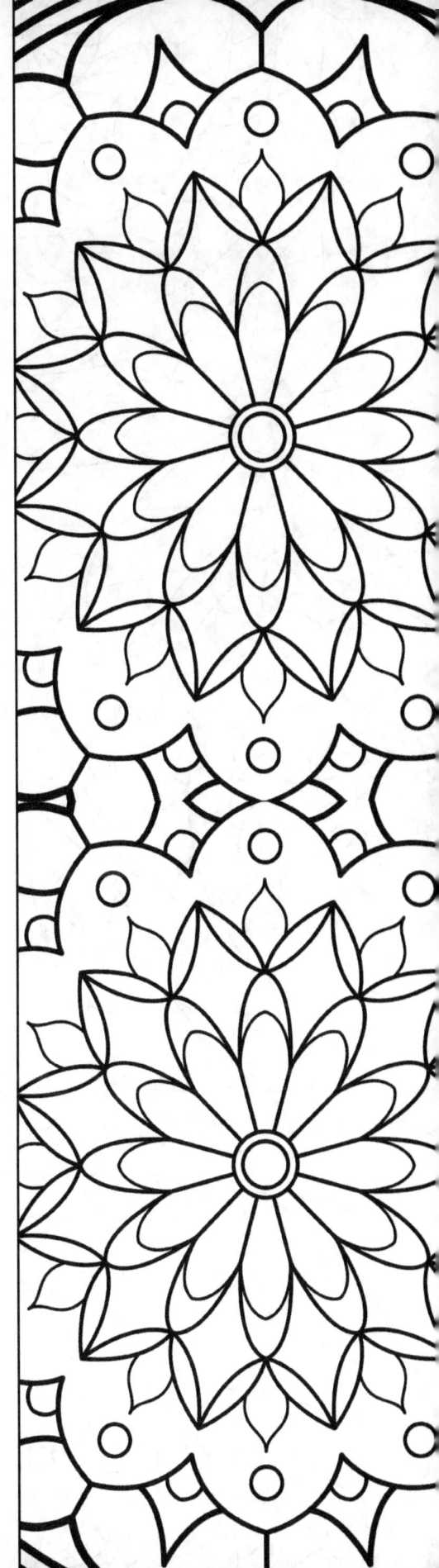

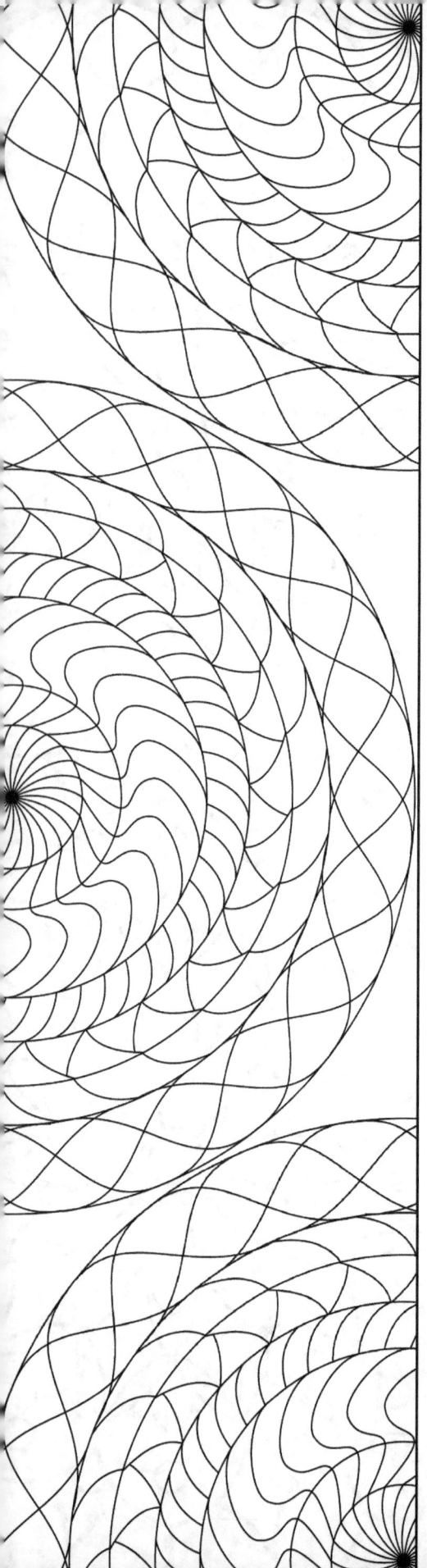

Make Swatches of Your Pencil Set

While this may not seem like a logical first step in the coloring process, making swatches of your colors helps you in many ways. A set of swatch sheets can be very handy to have on hand, especially if you are working with different sets of pencils, or have a very large set by one brand. During the process of swatching your colors, you can identify colors you like best and are easiest to use.

Familiarize Yourself with the Hues

Each colored pencil set is different. Some might have more greens and browns, some might have more red or blue. By sitting down with your pencils, you will learn about the colors. Within a single set, you might have a "favorite" hue because it simply appeals to your taste. Between sets, you might find that in head-to-head comparisons, some pencils perform better than others.

Learn the "Real" Color

Colored pencil companies often put color on the barrel, or outside of the pencil. While these colors might be close, or even a nearly perfect color match, the color on the outside of the pencil is often quite different that the lead inside. By making color swatches, you will be able to select your colors with more accuracy.

Easily Compare Different Sets and Brands

I recommend setting up a consistent order for how you make your swatch charts. If you have four sets of pencils, for instance, begin all of your swatch sheets with the same color. You might choose to begin with red, using the classic rainbow order. Or, you might prefer to make your pencil swatches starting with your warmest or with the lightest value color first.

Develop a Feel for the Pigmentation

Each pencil, even if they are from the same set, has a different level of pigmentation. Some pencils are just duds, laying out very little color, or requiring a lot of pressure. On your swatch test, included notes of how much pressure you needed to achieve full saturation.

Tip: If your colored pencil collection is bigger than the number of squares to the right, you can use the extra blank pages at the back of the book to make more swatches.

Pencil Set Name _____

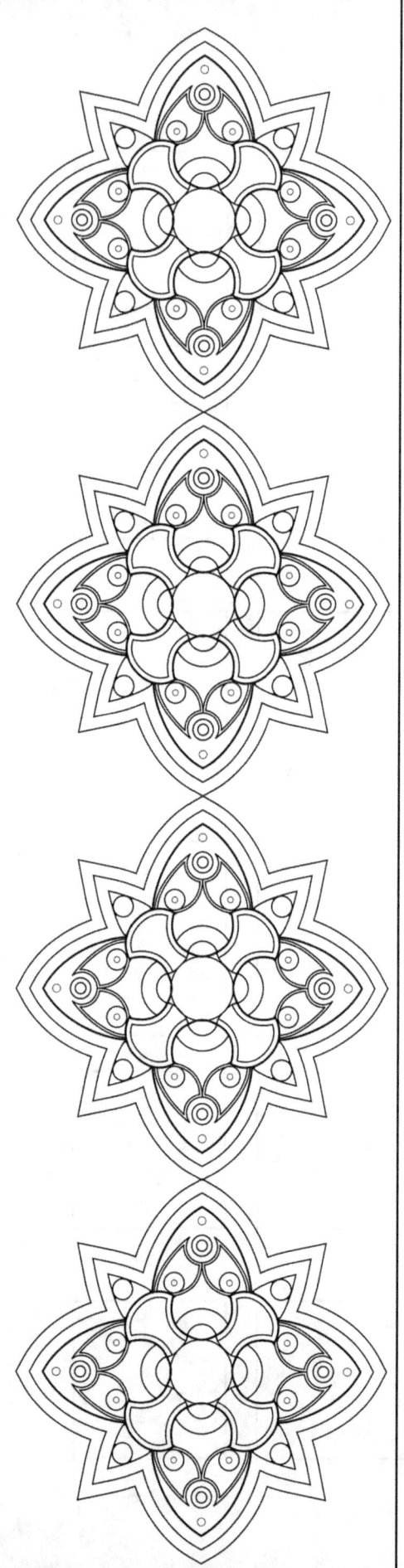

Working with Colored Pencils

Working with colored pencils takes practice and play. Take the time to really experiment and learn what techniques work best for you. Many devoted coloring book enthusiasts have created blog posts and video tutorials that address the many ways to color like an artist. Here are my top tips for improving your coloring skill and getting the best results in you finished pieces.

Think Like an Artist: Choose a Color Scheme

Before diving into a coloring book page, choose your colors ahead of time and pull out the pencils for your piece. Think like an artist or a chef and pull out the ingredients you will be using. It will save time while you are coloring and help you stay within a limited palette.

Experiment on the Duds

It goes without saying that not every coloring page in every coloring book will appeal to your taste and style. Every coloring book is different, and the quality of the paper can greatly impact your finished results. I recommend using your least favorite pages to experiment with pressure, stroke and grip with your pencil sets. Then, when you are ready to color a page you really love, you will know the quality of the paper from your experience practicing.

Vary your Grip

Take the time to learn to vary the way you hold your pencil in your hand. Most people start out holding their pencil in the standard tripod grip used for writing. But try to vary the angle you hold the pencil. Think about how you would hold your pencil to use the whole side of the tip.

Learn to Control Your Pressure

Mastery over the amount of pressure you use while coloring will help you master the art of blending and making fine gradations in value from light to dark. The key is always to build up from light to dark in light layers to build the exact hue and tone that you desire. You will also do much less sharpening if you use a light touch, especially when using softer pencils.

Experiment with Different Stroke Styles

The tip of the pencil can meet the paper at different angles to create different styles of strokes. Hatching, cross hatching, stippling and scumbling are different strokes that create different effects in the coloring process. There are many more so play with your pencils. Experiment and build a repertoire of methods to choose from in your coloring process.

Sharpen Frequently

Don't let wood accidently drag through your color or use a wide rounded point when you need precision. Stop and sharpen frequently.

Blending Colors

When working with colored pencils, the goal for mixing shades is to work in light layers to lay down different hues, as you build up the saturation of the pencil marks on the paper. The key to achieving smooth blends is to practice with your pencils. If you enjoy the look of a smoothly blended surface, you might want to invest in specialty blending products like a paper stump or tortillion that help you buff and blend.

Using a Blender Pencil

Another way to blend your colors is to use a colorless blending pencil. If you like the hue and values you've achieved, a colorless pencil, which is essentially just wax and binding medium, will blend your work without adding more color.

Blend with a Solvent

A clear blending marker is a great way to blend color pencil. It can create a smooth, almost painted effect by melting the wax and allowing the pigment to move more fluidly. Try an alcohol-based marker for best reults.

Burnishing

Once you've completed your coloring project, you can take it to the next level by burnishing. This is the process of going over your entire piece to reach maximum saturation, and a smooth, waxy finish the shine. To create a burnished finish over your piece, use a colorless blending pencil and small circular motions to buff the surface.

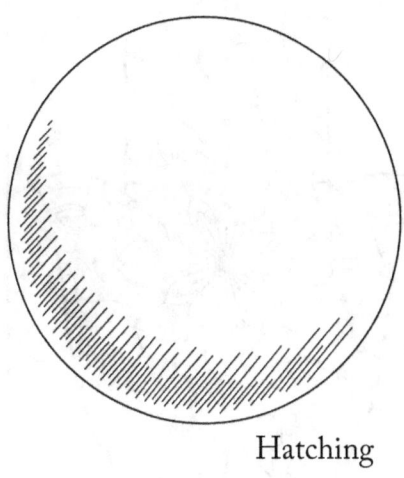

Hatching

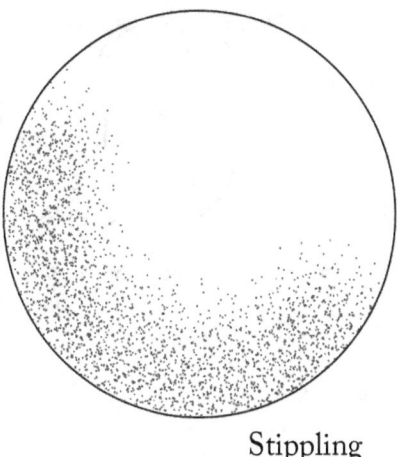

Stippling

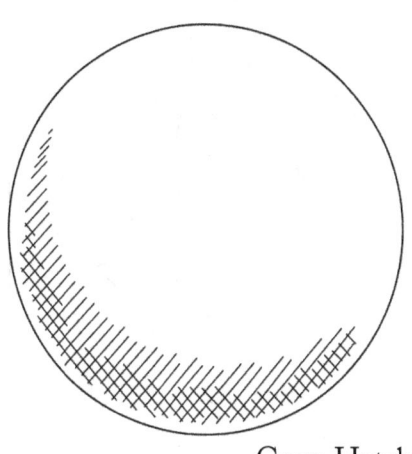

Cross Hatching

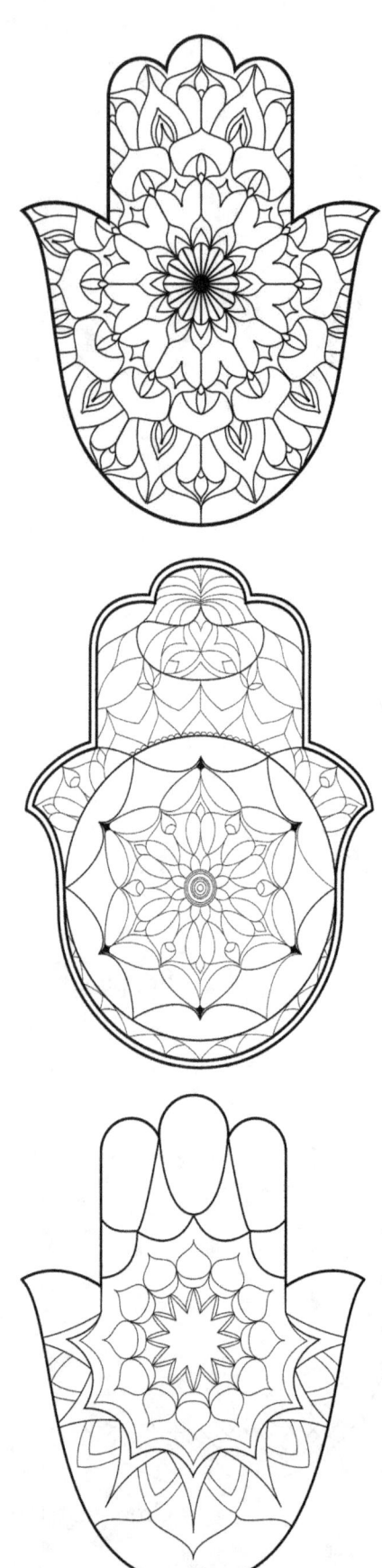

Practice and Play

The next pages are filled with mandalas and other geometric patterns and designs to use as you experiment with color.

Visual Research
As you read the inspirational prompts, take a moment to do some research to find examples of the same type of object to see how colors have been used in the past. You can find images in magazines, books, and online.

Pick a Color Scheme
Alternately, you can select a color scheme to try from the list of color harmonies on page 16. There are enough designs to practice all the color schemes multiple times until you find the ones that you like the most, and suit your taste and style.

Learn More Online
This brief introduction to design and color is just a beginning. If you find yourself wanting more information about design and color, we've included a selected reading list at the back of the book. However, there is a tremendous amount of free information available online in articles, blogs and video form.

Practice
If you are just starting out with using colored pencils, allow yourself time to practice your technique. The more you color, the more familiar you become with your tools. Make time to develop your design skills by choosing color schemes and coloring them in. Don't have enough time? Only color half a design.

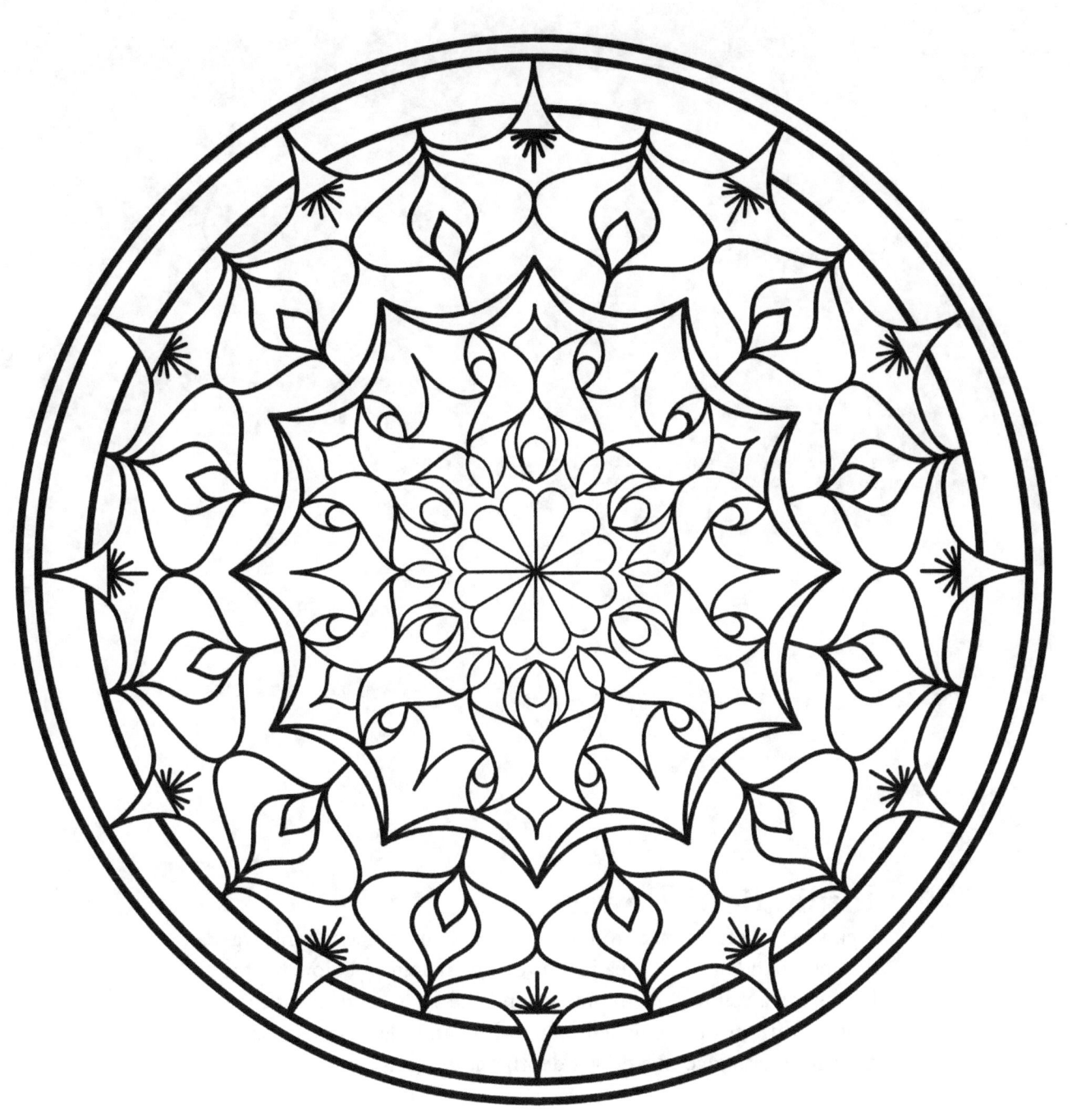

Inspiration: Flowers

Pick your favorite flower to inspire your color choice for this traditional mandala. One idea is to use two analogous colors for the flower, say a yellow and an orange, and then add a green for the leaves. With just three pencils, plus white and black, create variations in hue to give this flower depth and dimension.

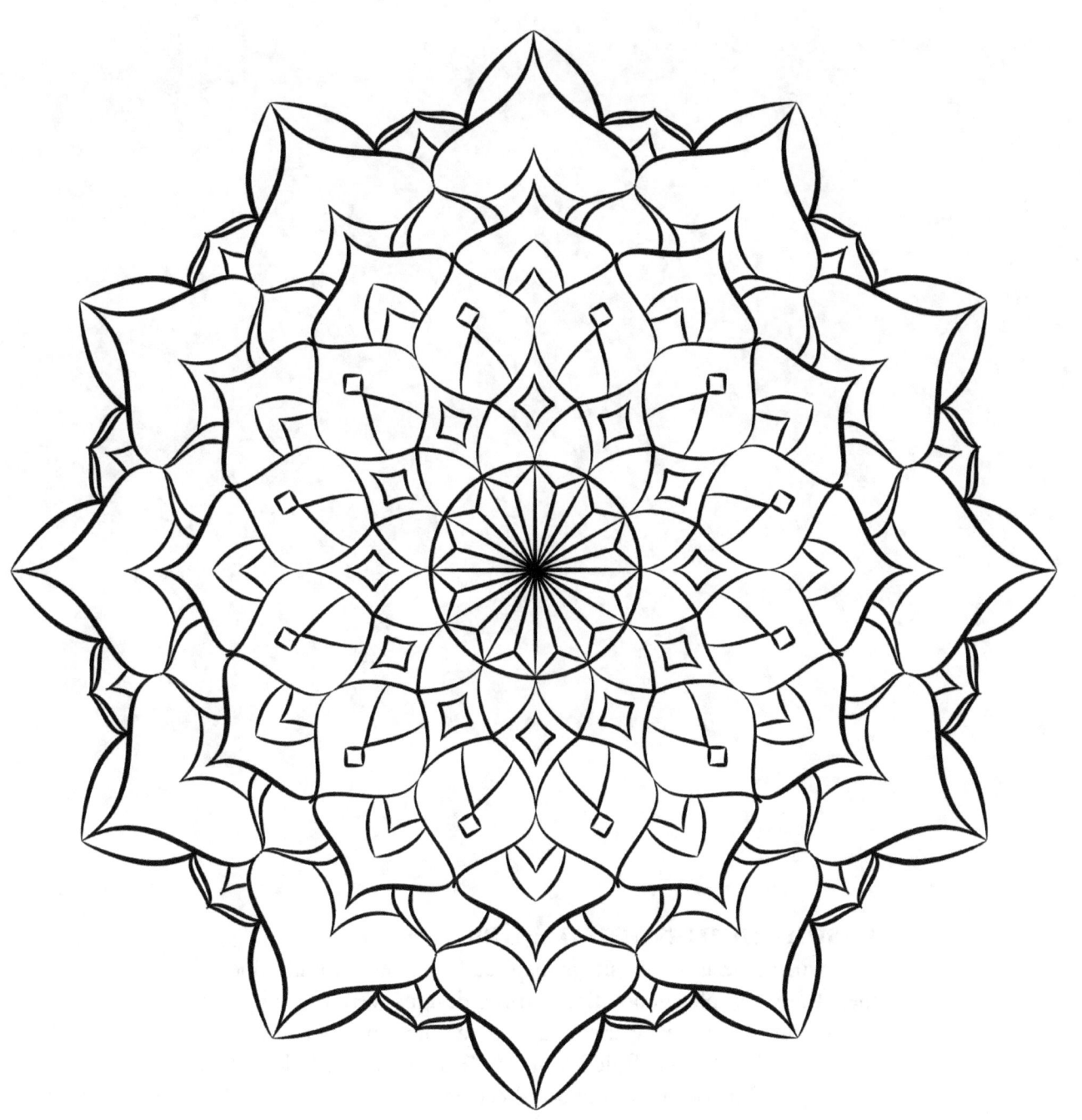

Inspiration: Roman Tiles

The swirling design opposite is inspired by ancient Roman floor tiles. These complex geometric swirling designs were very popular in the homes of wealthy aristocrats. Do a quick internet search using terms like "Ancient Tile Floors" or "Roman Tile Work" to look at images of the originals and use those colors to guide your color choices.

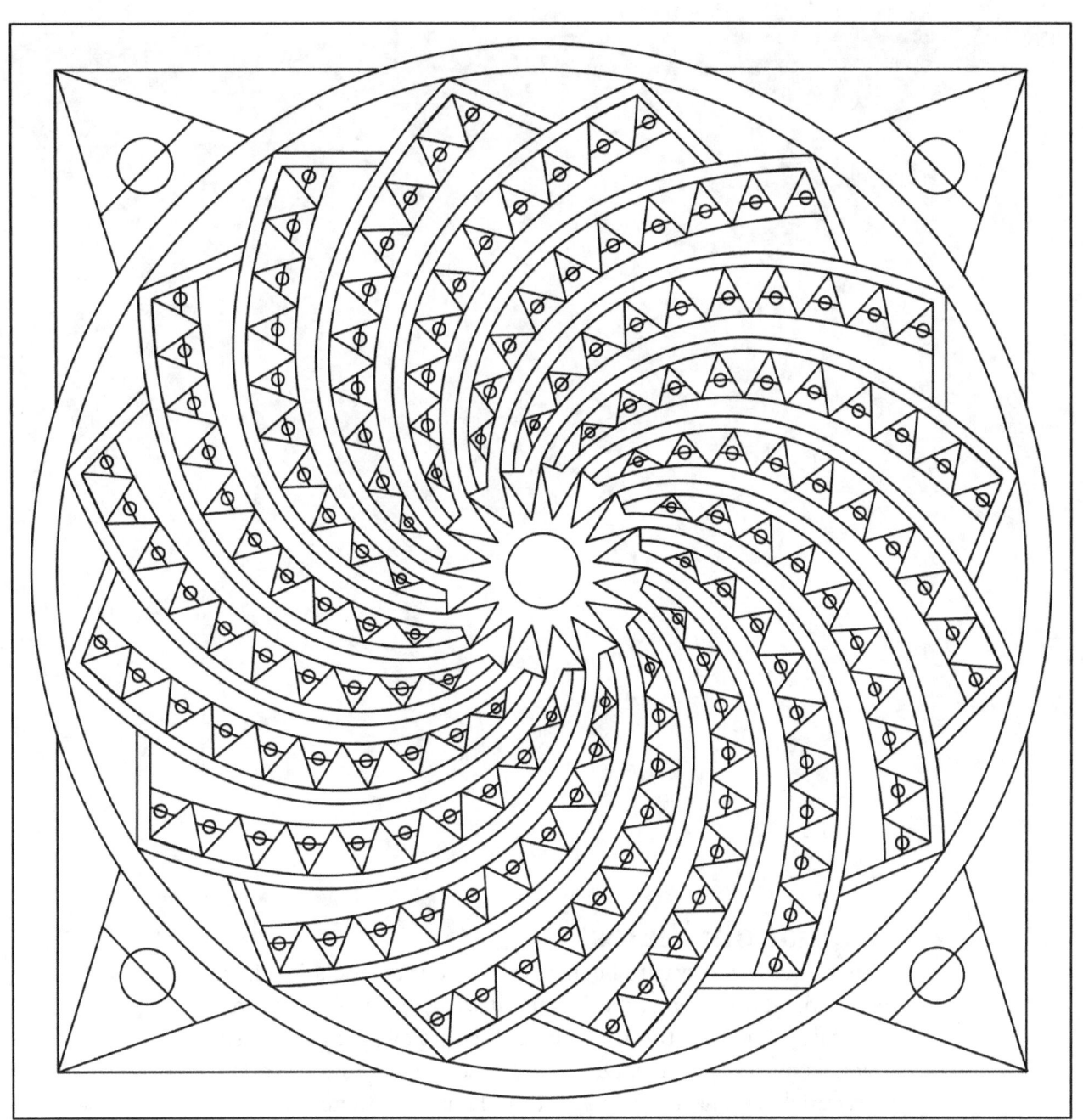

Inspiration: Plates

Perhaps the easiest way to be inspired for your color choices is to look at the illustration and think about what this image reminds you of. If you look at this drawing and see a plate, then seek inspiration from similar items. Dinner plates are made from all sorts of materials, and have been used for millennia, so there is a rich source of images for your inspiration, from modern home-goods catalogs to museum collections.

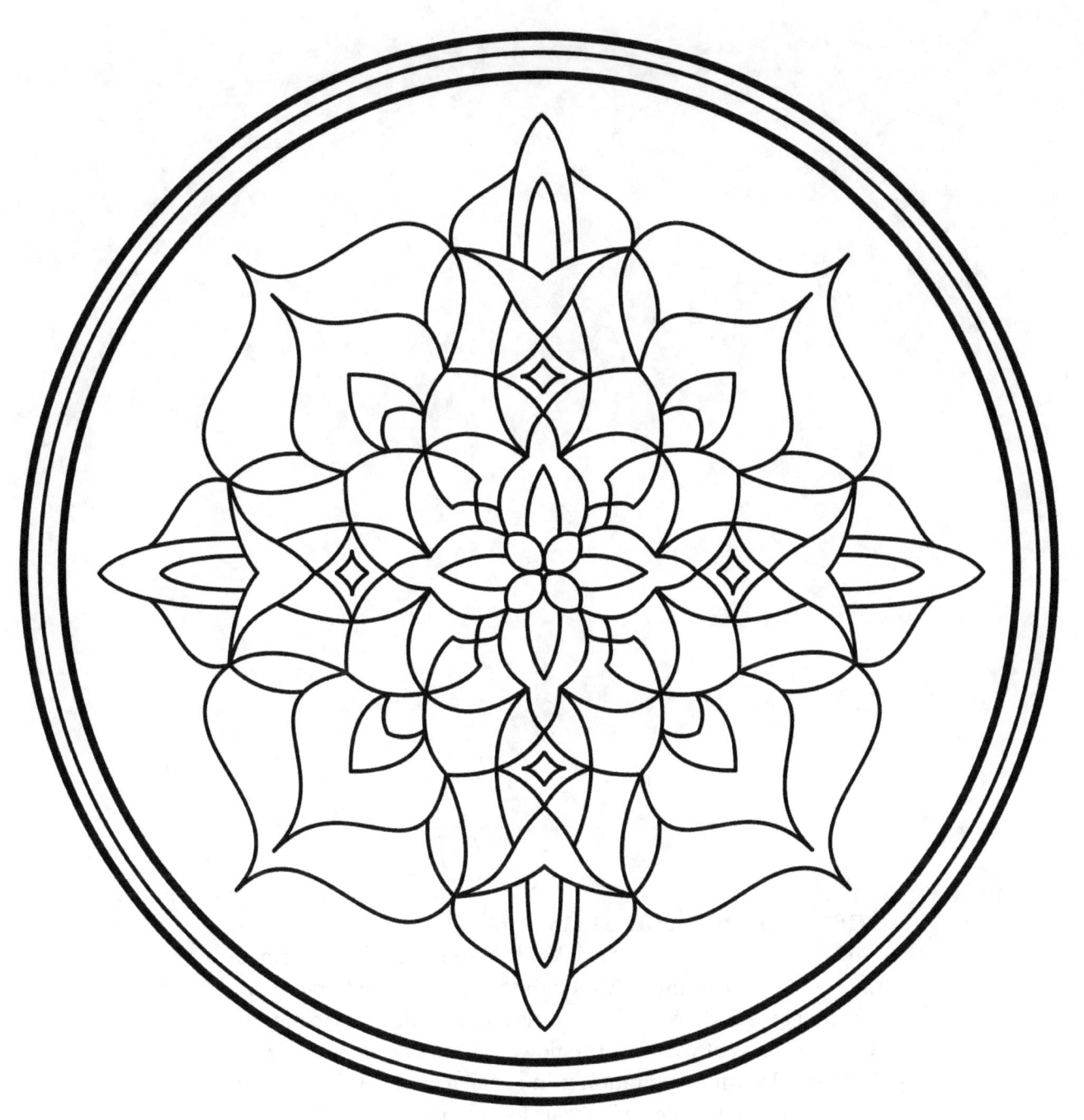

Inspiration: Gardens

Flowers, trees, and plants of all kinds have inspired artists since the era of cave paintings. Although this is the same floral design repeated over and over, think of this like a garden and experiment with the colors of your favorite flowers. One of the places designers like to look for inspiration is in actual gardens. If it's not convenient to visit a garden, visit your local library and look up books about gardening, landscaping, and even flower arranging!

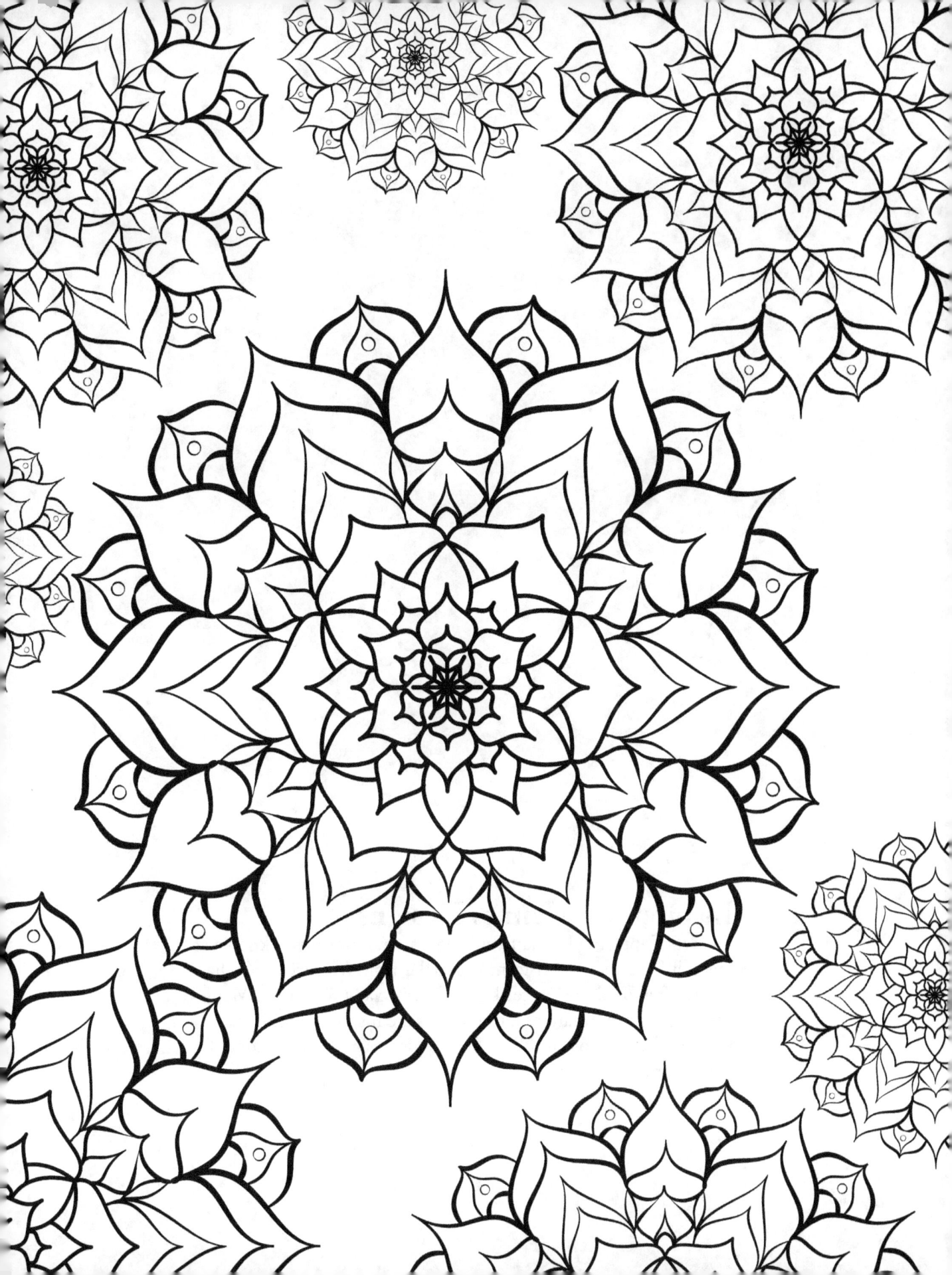

Inspiration: Mehndi Designs

The art of applying henna to create temporary tattoos is known as mehndi. This ancient art form is popular from Morocco to India, and is often used during celebrations, especially weddings. Many contemporary permanent tattoo artists are inspired by this long tradition, and choose to fill mehndi-style designs with shades of grey or brilliant color.

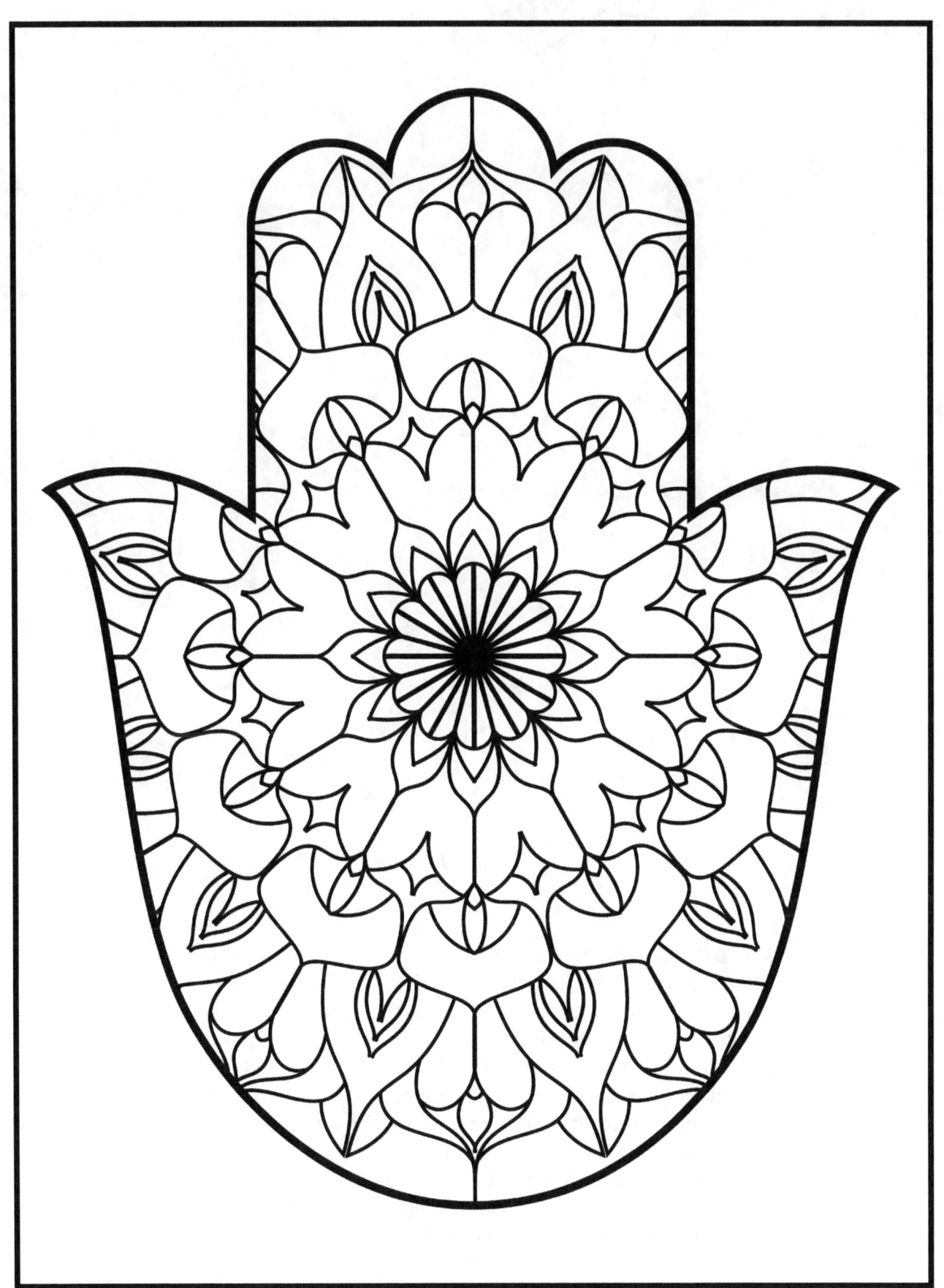

Inspiration: Art Deco

Often drawings start one way, and finish in a different design space. I started out drawing a traditional floral motif, but after the inner rings, the pattern started to look decidedly art deco. This was an art movement that simplified and stylized designs to create clean bold lines and broad expanses of color. Art deco color schemes were often high contrast with lots of deep tones like brown, burgundy, and black paired with their lighter counterparts of tan, pink, and grey. Metallic tones were used in abundance as highlights. Heavy blending and burnishing can hint at the sheen of metal to gold, copper, and grey toned pencils.

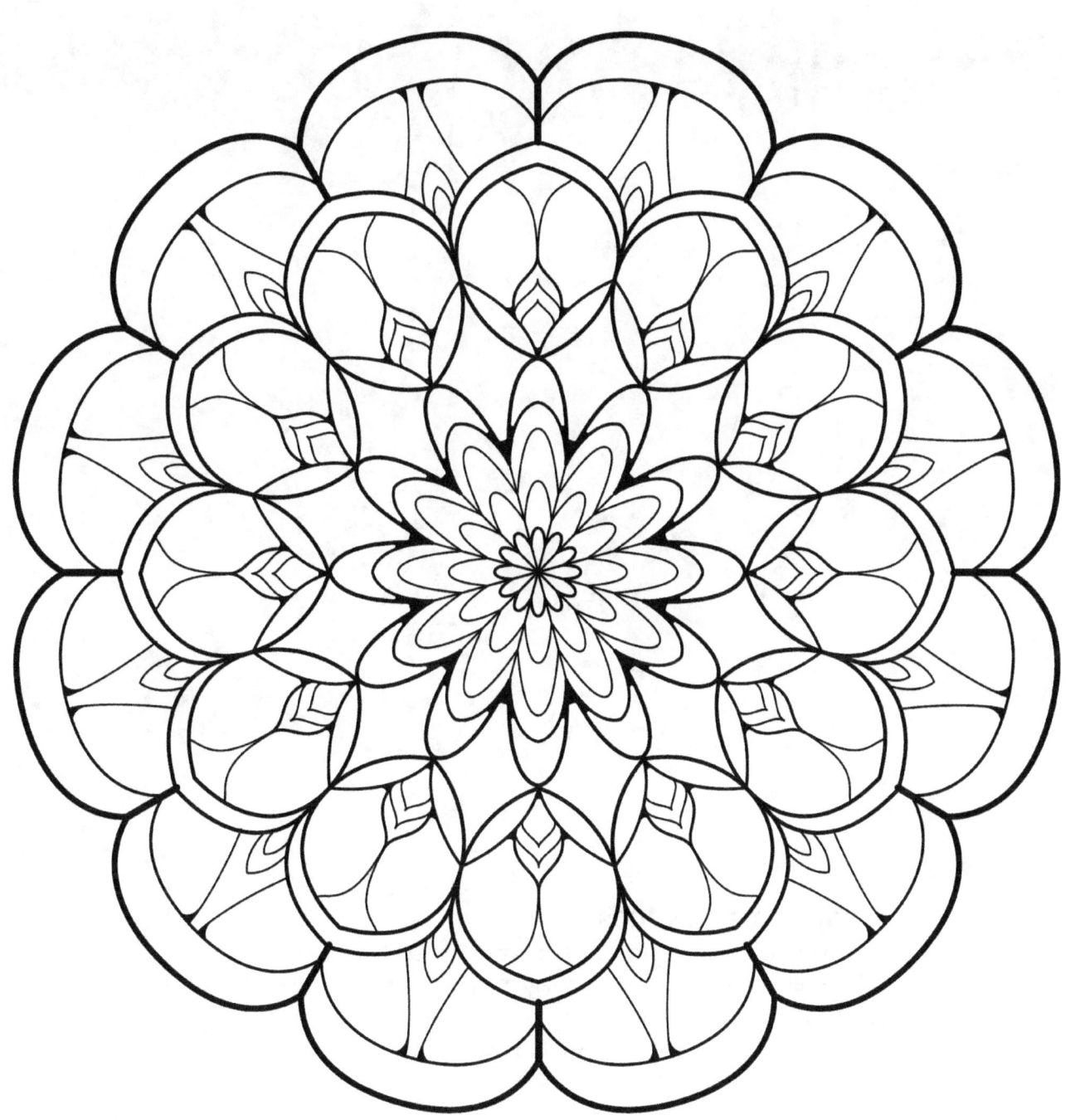

Inspiration: Ocean

This mandala was inspired by the ocean, sea shells, and waves. However, when I shared this image with a few friends, several of them saw candy or ice cream cones. As the artist, you get to choose which direction you would like to take a piece.

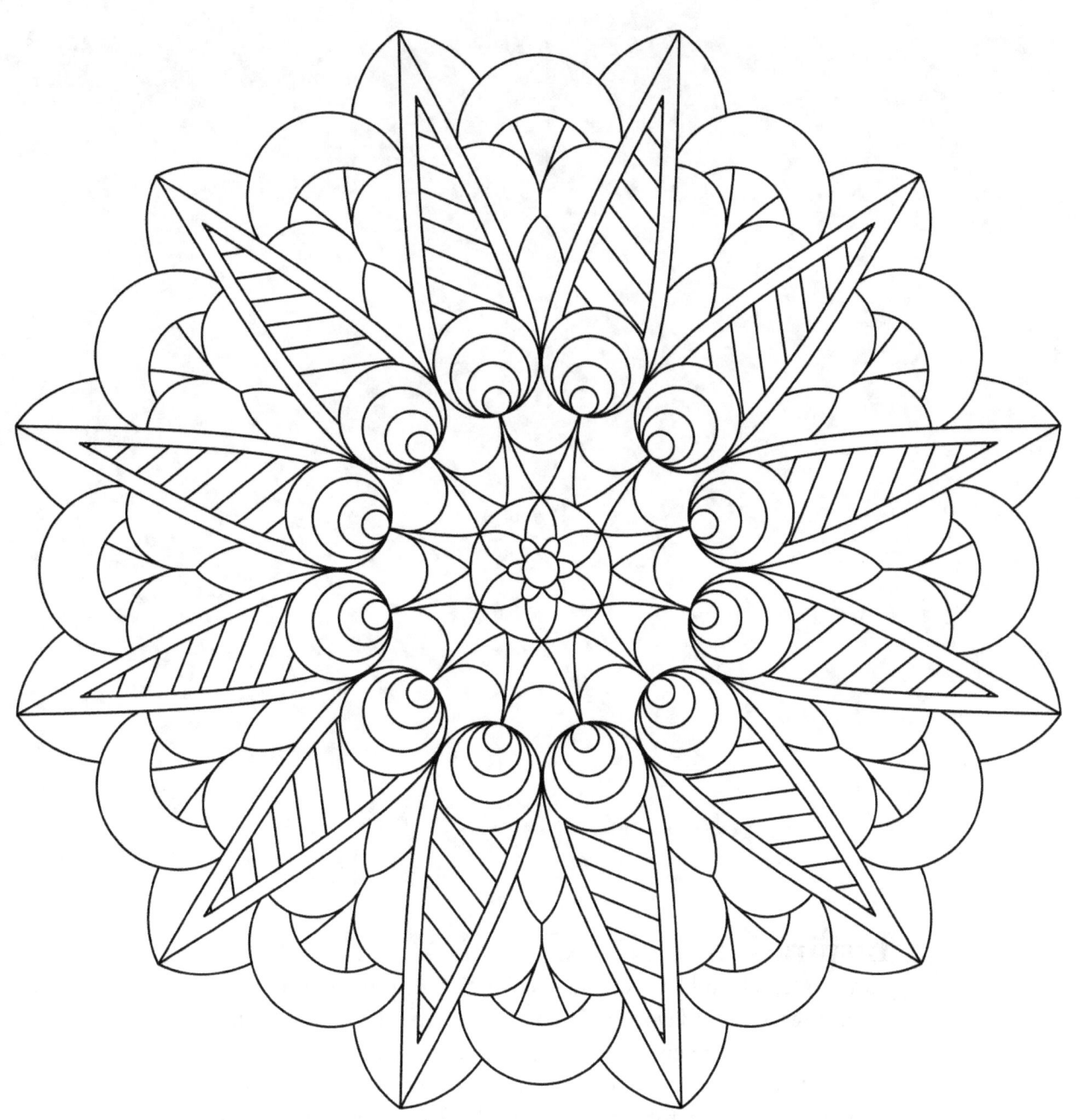

Inspiration: Celtic Church Windows

I love to travel, and I have a huge collection of photos from my adventures. One of favorite places to visit when I'm traveling to other countries, are churches, shrines and holy places of the region. This particular design is loosely based on a design from a Gothic church I visited in while touring the UK. A good source for color schemes for Celtic or Gothic designs are illuminated manuscripts.

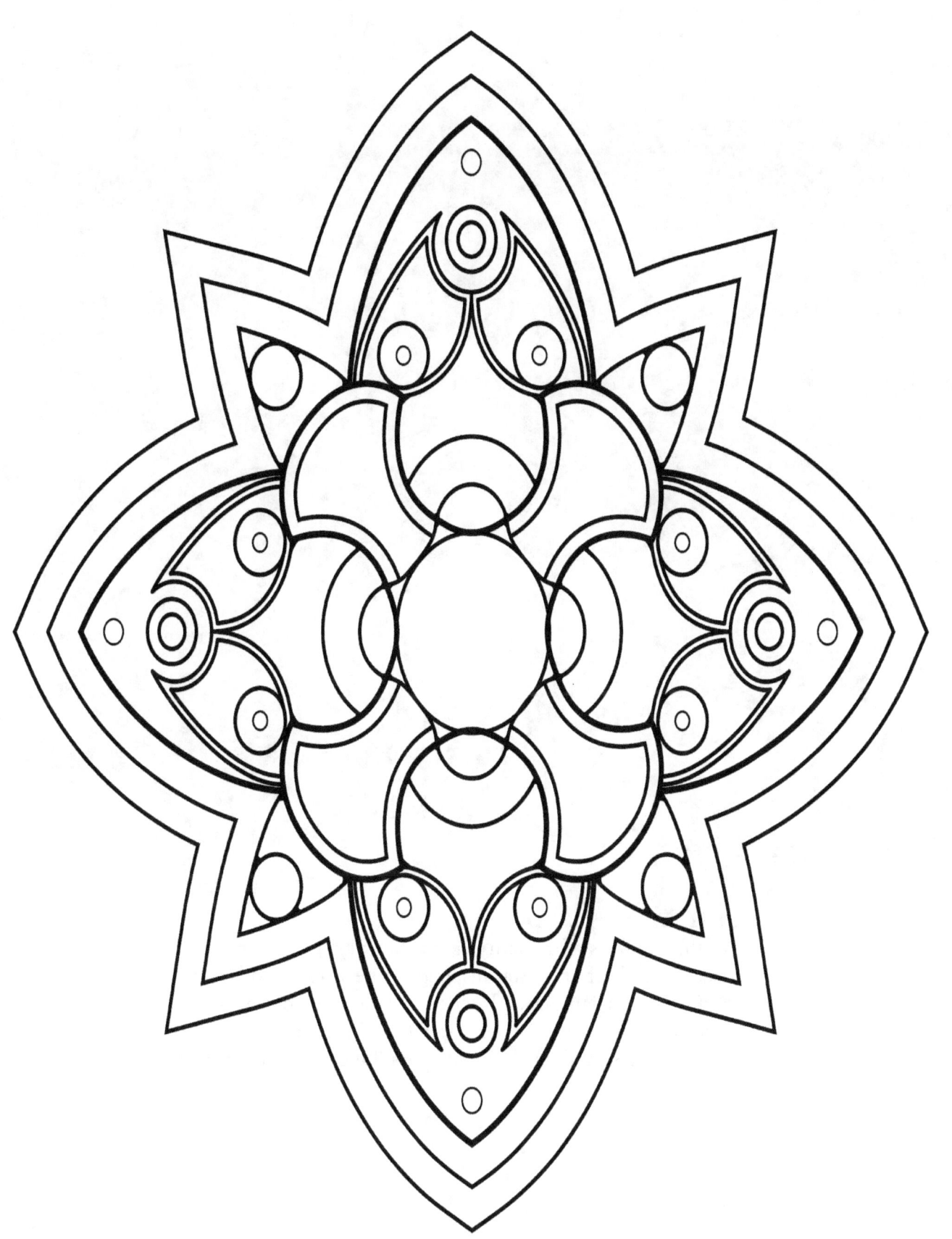

Inspiration: Carpet

One of the comforts of modern living is thick luxurious carpet underfoot. This illustration was inspired by the shapes and layouts of a traditional Persian carpet. Interior designers will often use a magnificent carpet as a source of inspiration for an entire room. Consider what colors your ideal room would include and use them in this design.

Inspiration: Flowers

When you look downward into many flowers, like daisies, lotuses, and roses, you will see the rows of radiating petals and leaves that inspire round designs. The world is filled with beautiful flowers of virtually every hue. What flower does this design remind you of? Or, you can create your own fantasy flower and let your imagination guide your color choice.

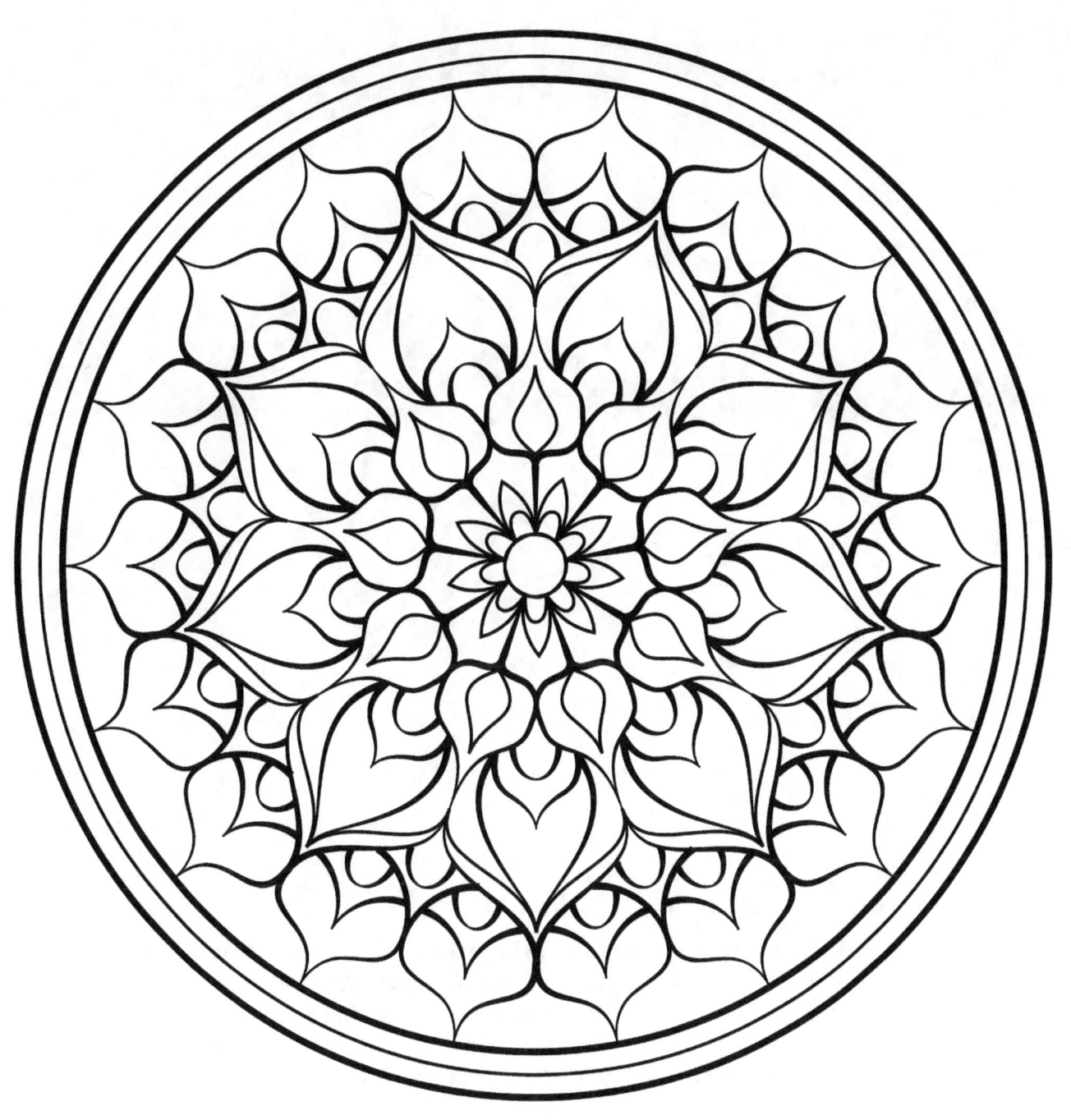

Inspiration: Kaleidoscope

Kaleidoscopes were invented in 1816, an entertaining device that used mirrors, pieces of glass or crystal, and light to create a brilliant optical experience. The mirrors create a repeating pattern. As you choose your colors for this piece, be sure to color all of the repeats the same color to create the kaleidoscopic effect.

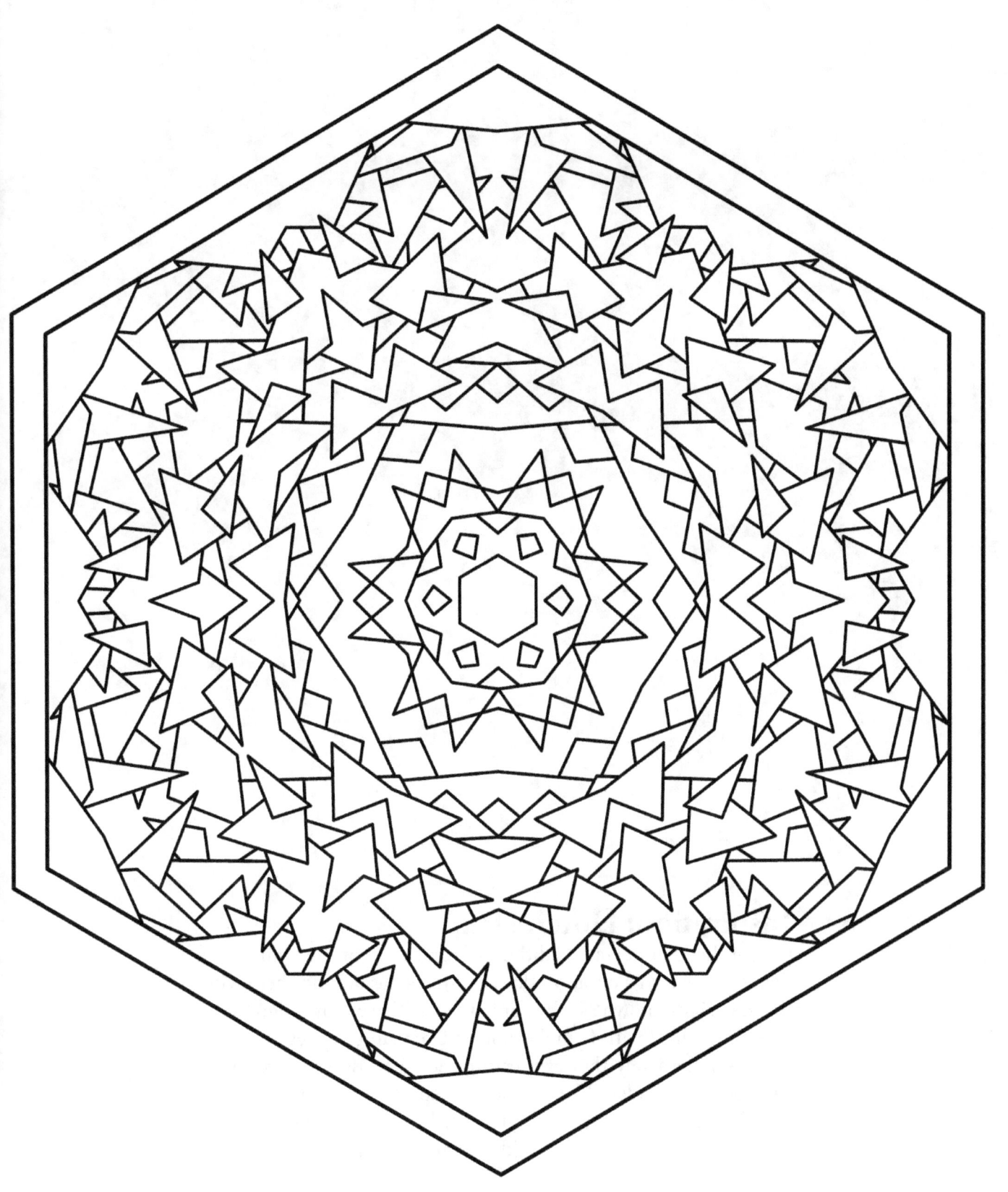

Inspiration: Dutch Hex

One of the art and craft traditions of rural areas of the United
States is to adorn a door, window, and the areas around them with
round designs known as a hex or barn star. These round signs are
sometimes filled with figural elements like plants, flowers and
animals. Alternately, they can feature geometric designs like com-
pass roses or mandala-like roundels of repeated patterns or stars.
The Dutch hex is closely associate with Pennsylvania folk arts and
frequently uses a bright and bold primary color scheme.

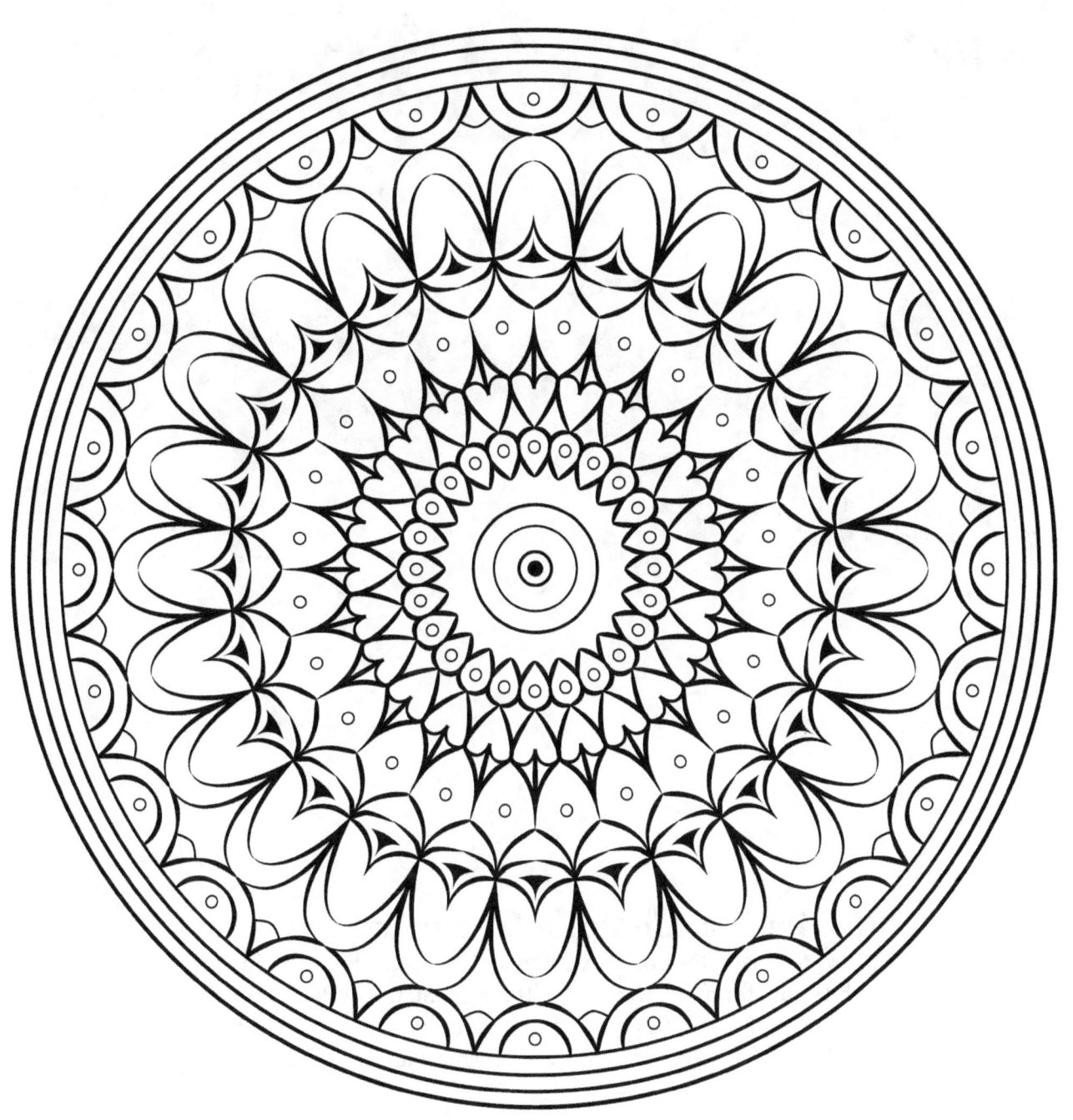

Inspiration: Complex Geometry

I love looking at the complex geometry of Islamic tile work in architecture from Spain to India. These geometric designs are built from repeating squares and circles, straight lines and arcs, to create tessellations, or repeated geometric designs with no overlaps and gaps.

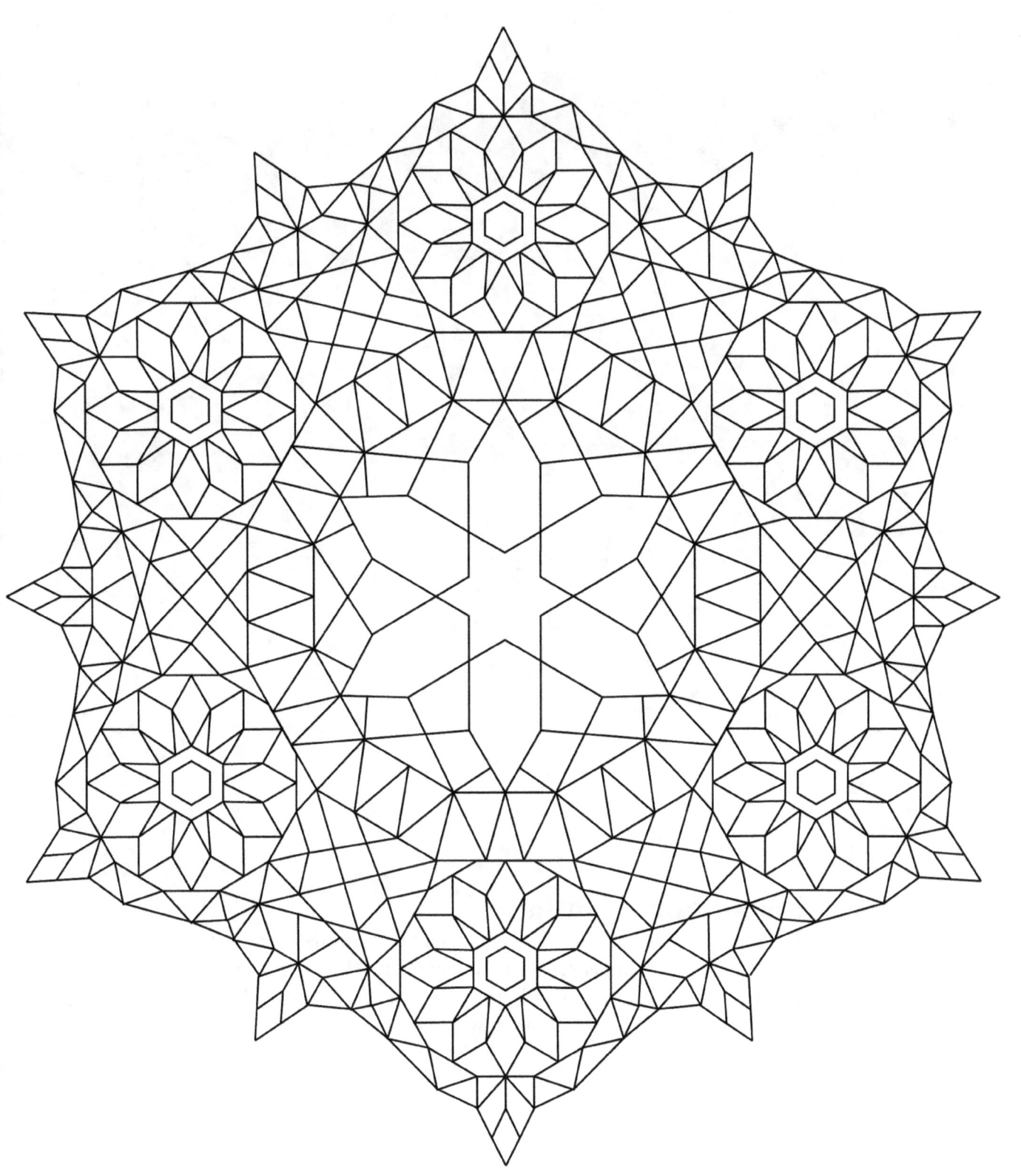

Inspiration: Hamsa

The hamsa or hand of Fatima, is an ancient pattern that originated in the middle east and is known by many names. This symbol is used to ward off bad spirits and protect against the evil eye. This Moroccan style hand was inspired by a doorknocker.

Inspiration: Geometric Line Art

When I was a little girl, I spent hours with my Spirograph® set and colored pens. I really enjoyed experimenting with the lines and the effects of different colored ballpoint pens. Often, after drawing my design, I would take colored pencils to fill them in. This mandala was inspired by those designs, and it inspires me to use nostalgic colors from my childhood.

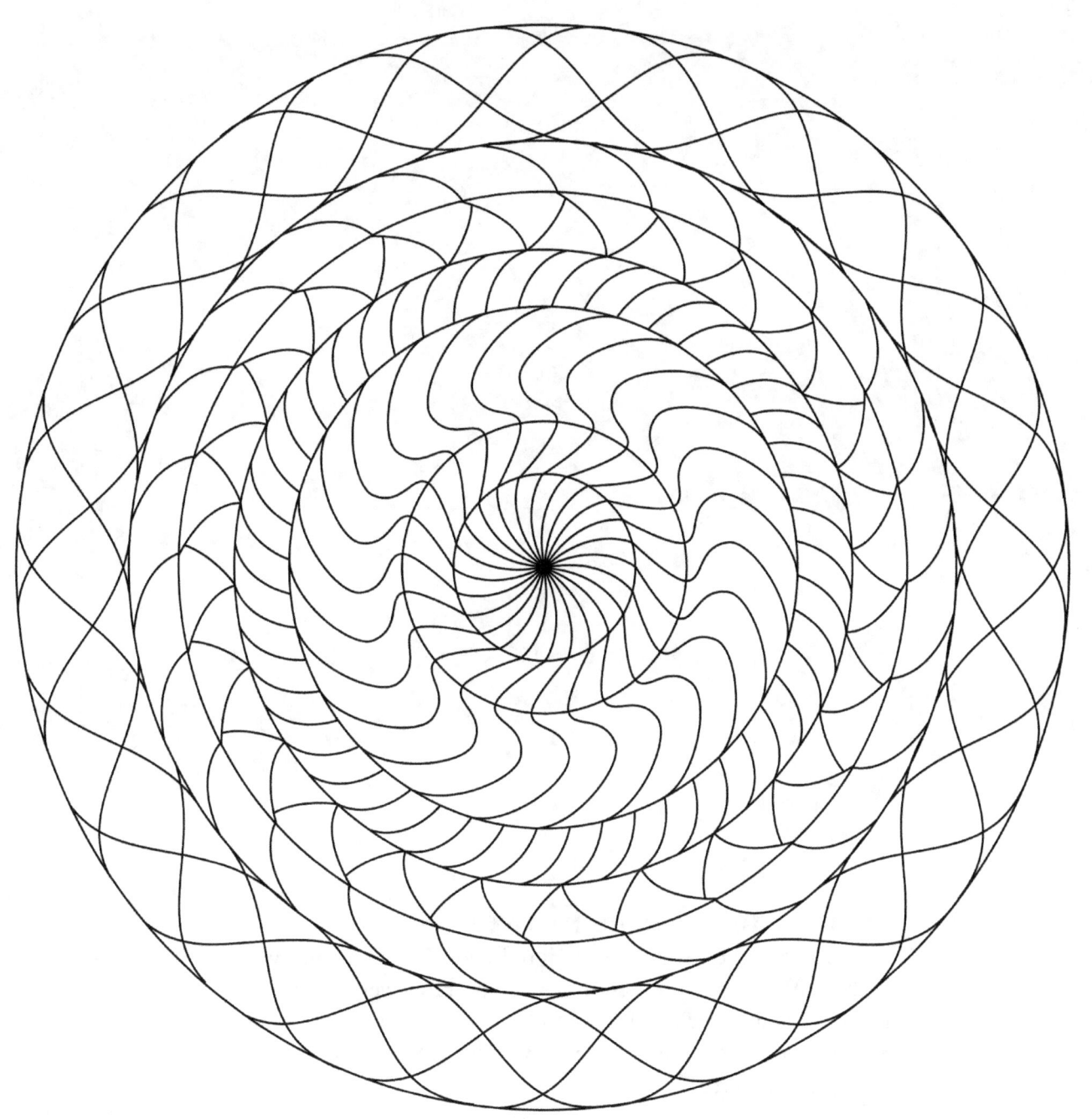

Inspiration: Lotus Flower

When I started drawing this design, I had in mind a color wheel, with each large petal representing a color. However, when drawing petal forms in a circle, it is easy to find yourself drawing a beautiful lotus flower, a sacred image in Buddhism that expresses balance through symmetry.

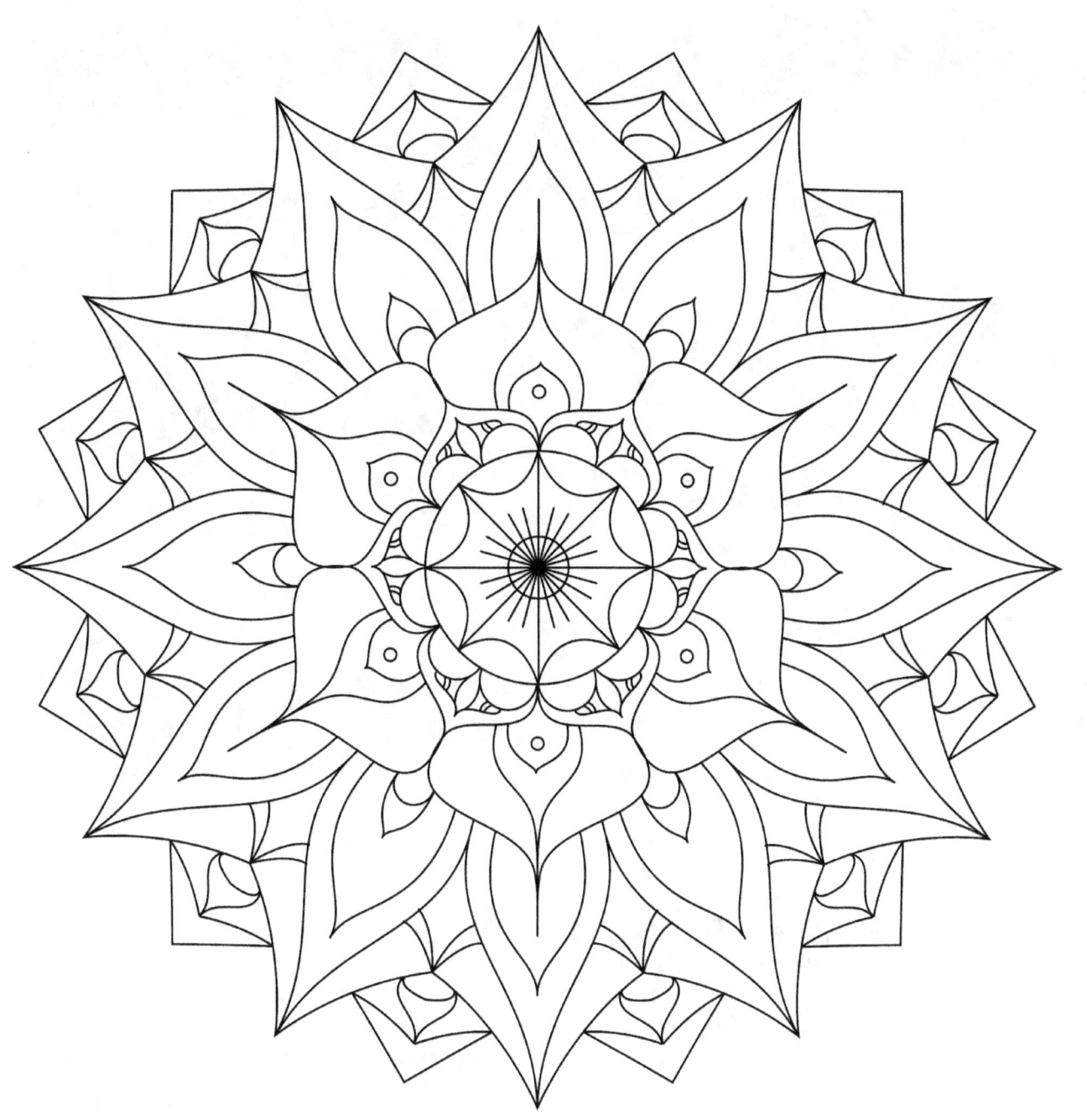

Inspiration: Playing Cards

Sometimes a design's color scheme is implied by the subject matter. In this design, the playing card motifs call for a red, black, and white, palette. Of course, modern playing cards come in a wide variety of colors, so you can let your imagination run wild!

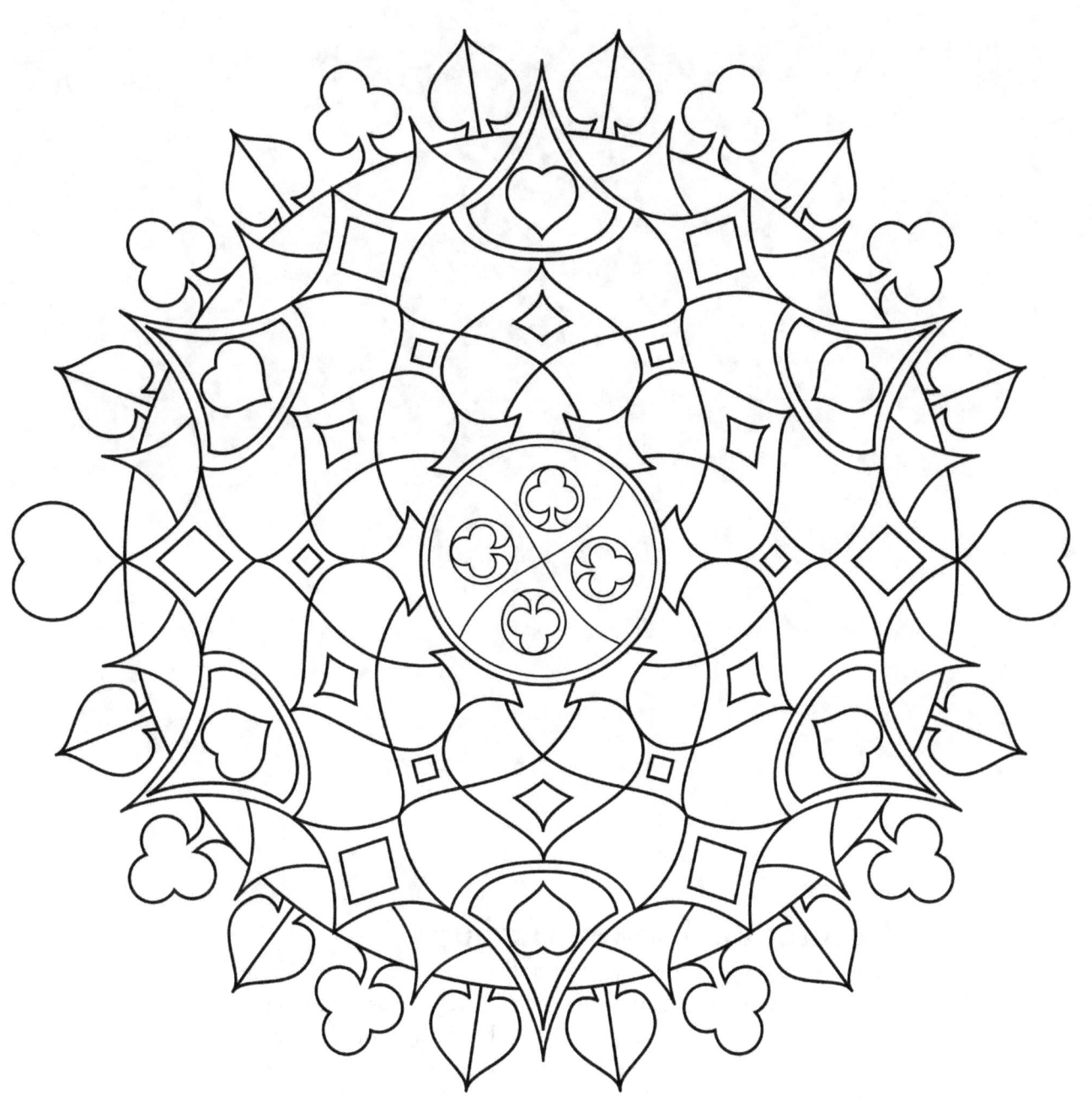

Inspiration: Flower Mashup

Sometimes you can see different motifs within a design. When I drew this original mandala, my pencil sketch was inspired by a sunflower. When George got hold of the illustration, he saw the tulip motif in the center, and decided to feature it in the border design. Placement of color will determine if you emphasize the tulips or use an analogous color scheme to create a beautiful sunflower.

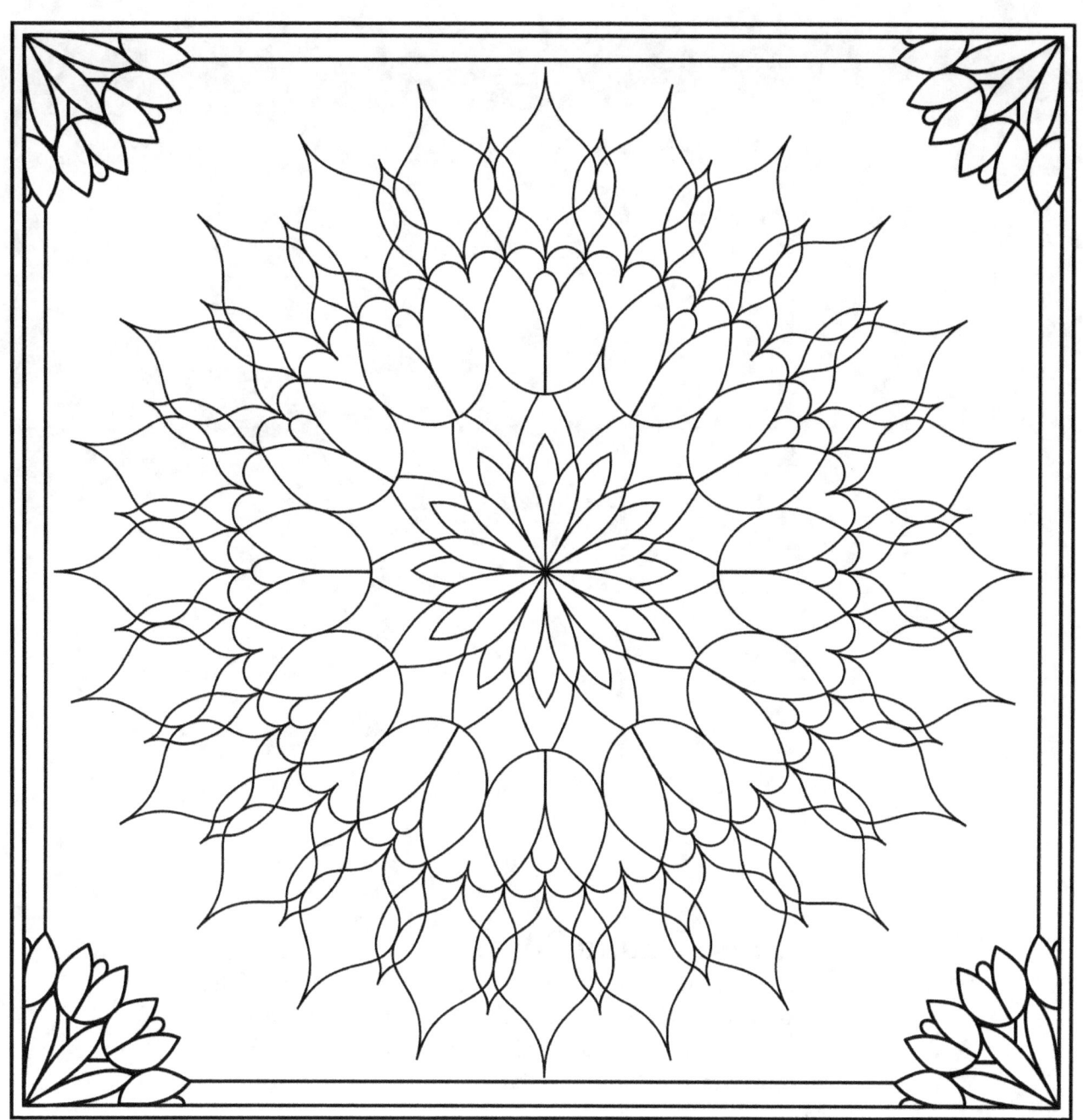

Inspiration: RoundTiles

This circular motif was inspired by Iznik pottery from Turkey. This region is known for it's pottery and tiles in bright vibrant turquoise, bright blue, crimson and white. Dating back to the 1500's, there are centuries of colorful inspirations to look at when coloring this page.

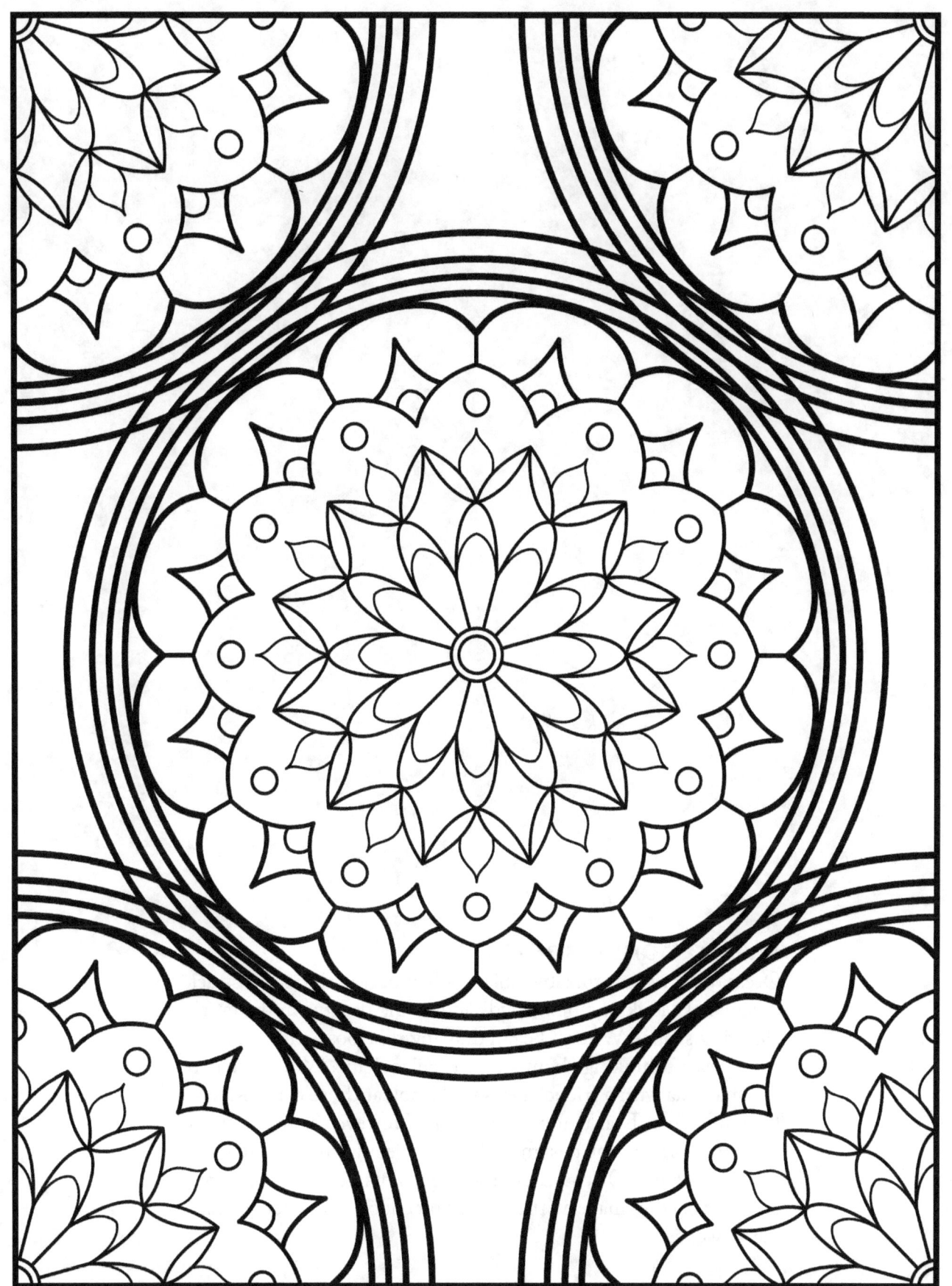

Inspiration: Candles

Occasionally, a recognizable object will appear within an abstract design. Like looking up at clouds and seeing designs in the ever changing shapes. When I began drawing this loose and open design, I wasn't thinking about any particular shape. When I shared this mandala with a friend they said, "Look at those candles." Now, of course, I can't stop seeing them. However, as an artist you can either play up the design with bright yellow and orange to represent flames. Or you could use cool colors in those spaces to erase the candle imagery. The colors you choose will decide what the viewer sees.

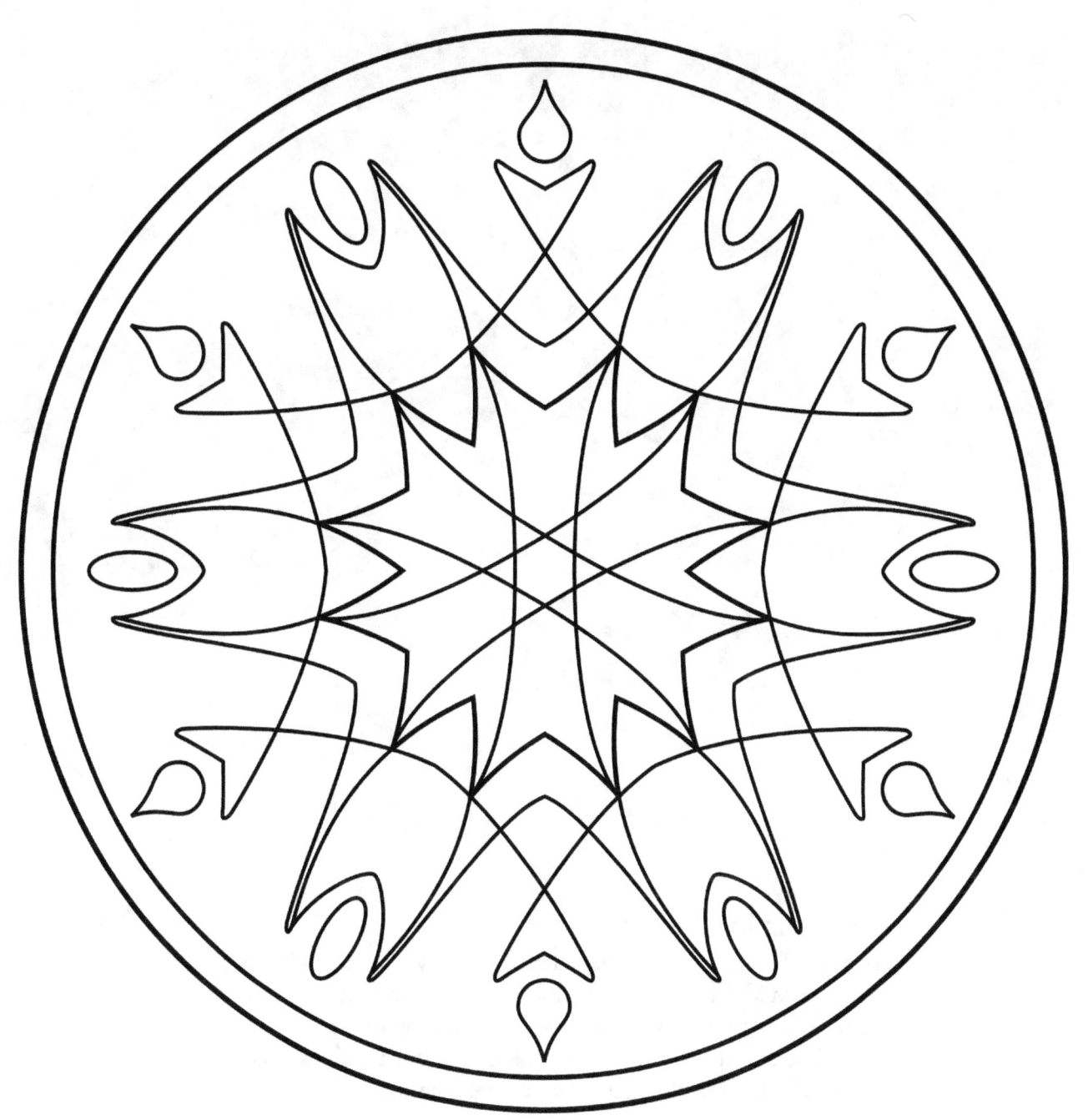

Inspiration: Ancient Art

This is a design based on an ancient Greek kyllx, or drinking cup. As one would drink wine, the design would come into view. Ancient pottery came in various teracotta colors, with black and red glaze. You can also take a more modern approach and use colors inspired by the Greek Islands like white, blue, and red.

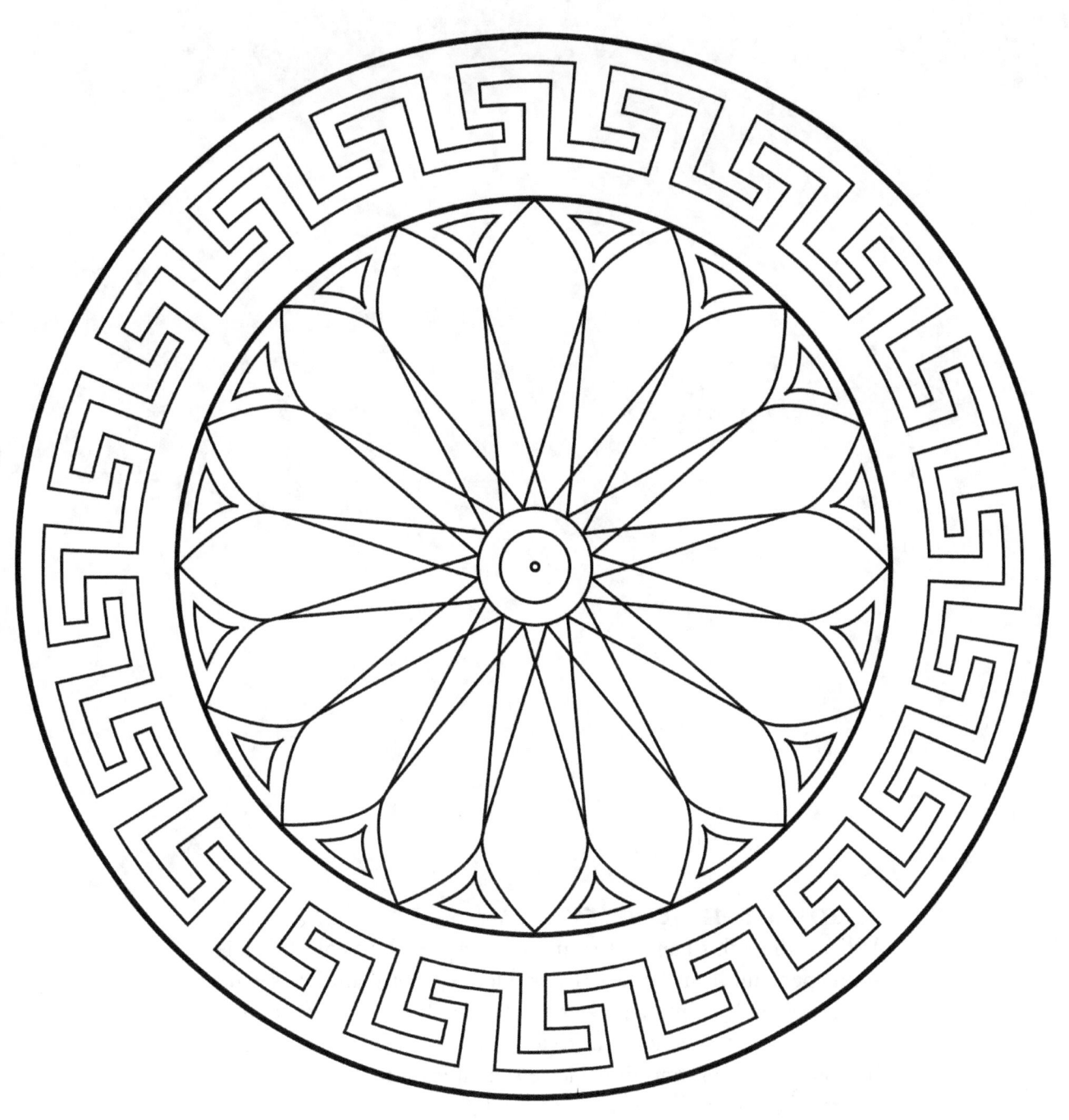

Inspiration: Jewelry

When I drew this hamsa design, I was inspired by a colorful cloisonné pendant from Turkey. It was filled with brilliant blues, reds, and golds, and set into a pewter-toned metal base. Before coloring in this design, take a moment to look at jewelry and make your hue selection from traditional jewelry materials such as the natural colors of gemstones or brightly colored glass.

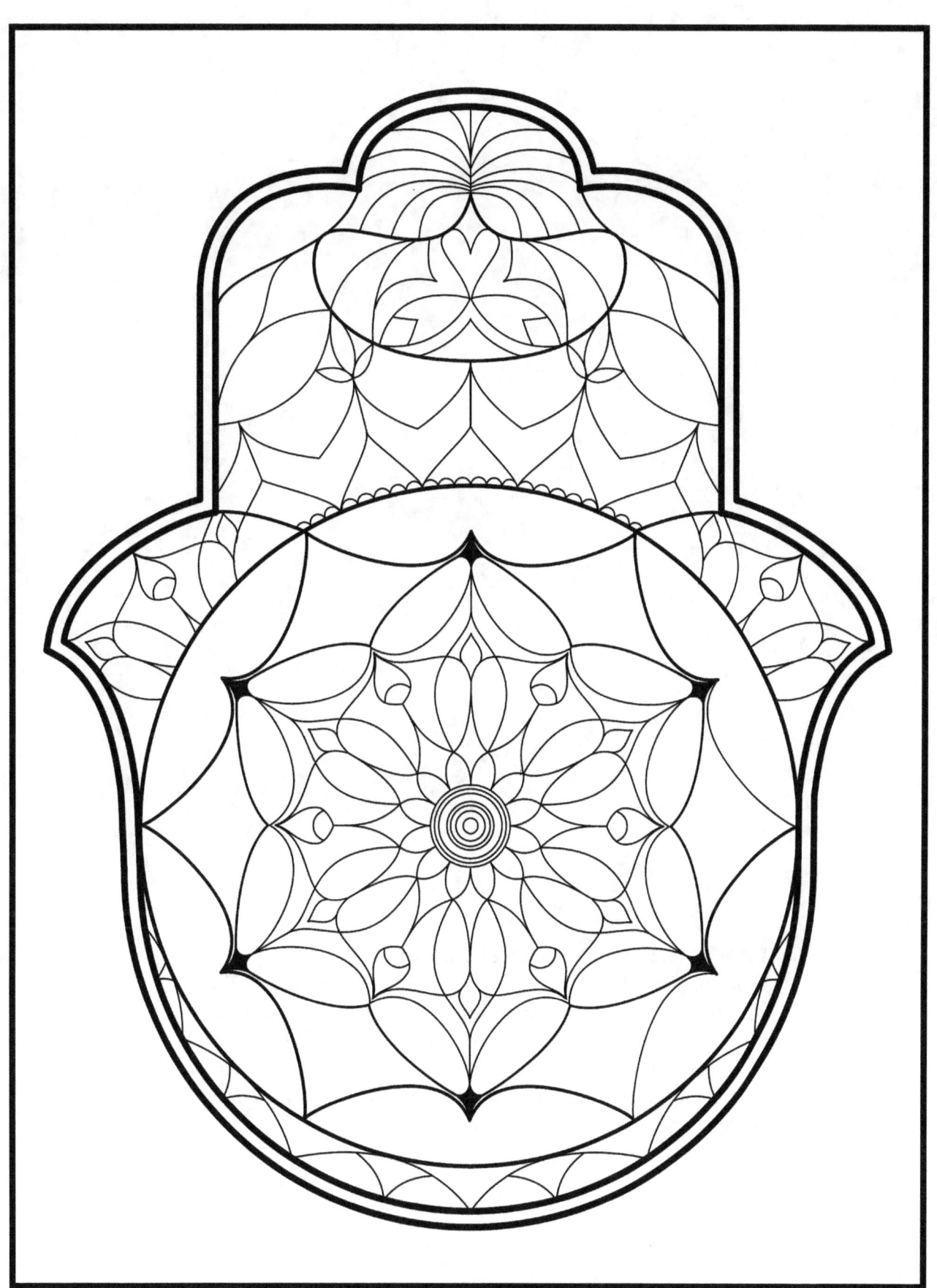

Inspiration: Straight Lines

When you are working with colored pencils, you can control the way you apply your color. In this mandala, why not experiment with laying down the colors you choose using visible lines that echo the straight lines of the design. Using your colors to reinforce the the movement and direction of your design lines may even create a sense of movement.

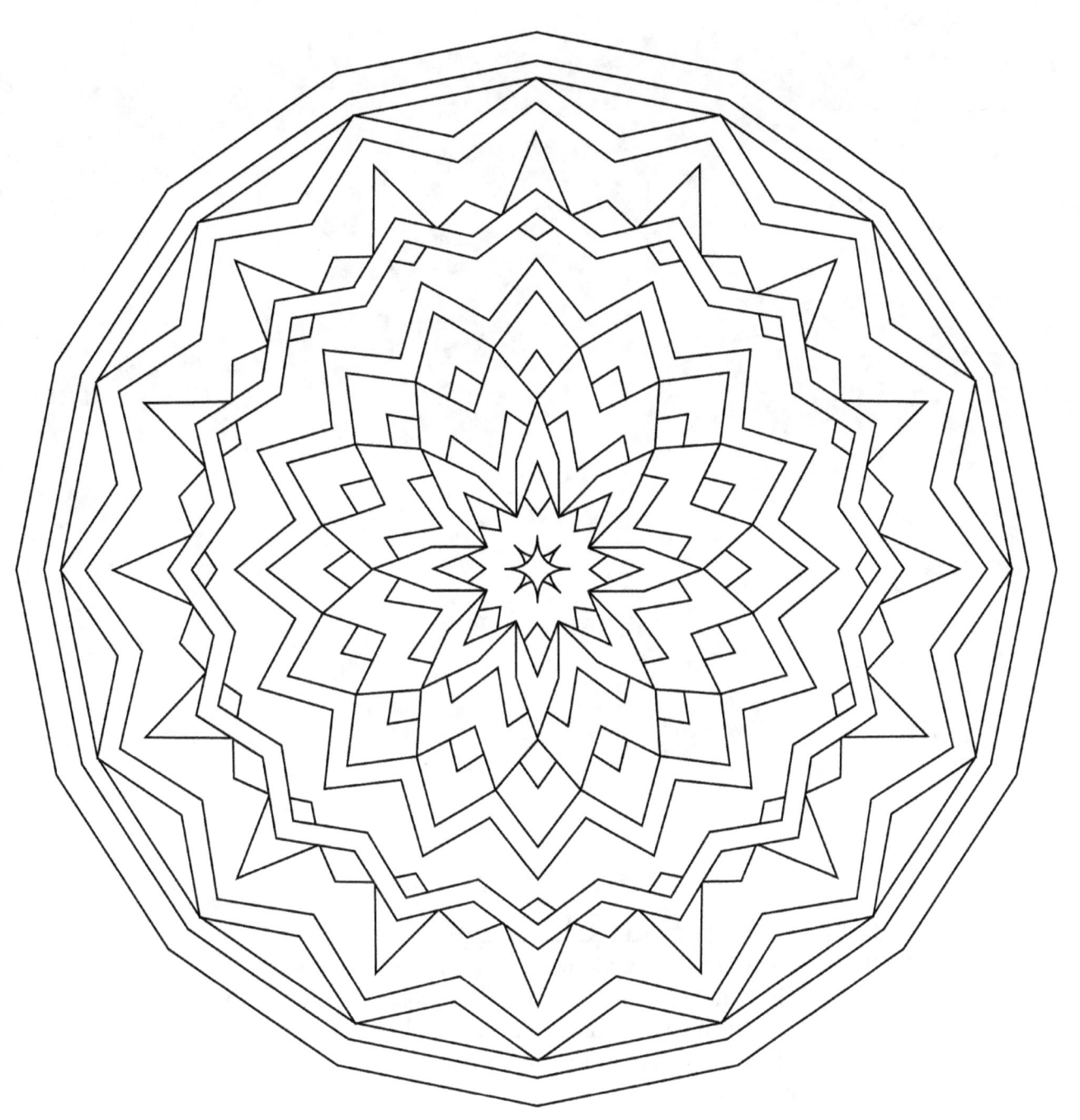

Inspiration: Four Blessings

This stylized symbol from China represents four blessings or virtues of life. These blessings include virtue, longevity, prosperity, and good health. This motif is used by fans and practitioners of the art of Fung Shui and is often hung as art to bring this positive energy into the home.

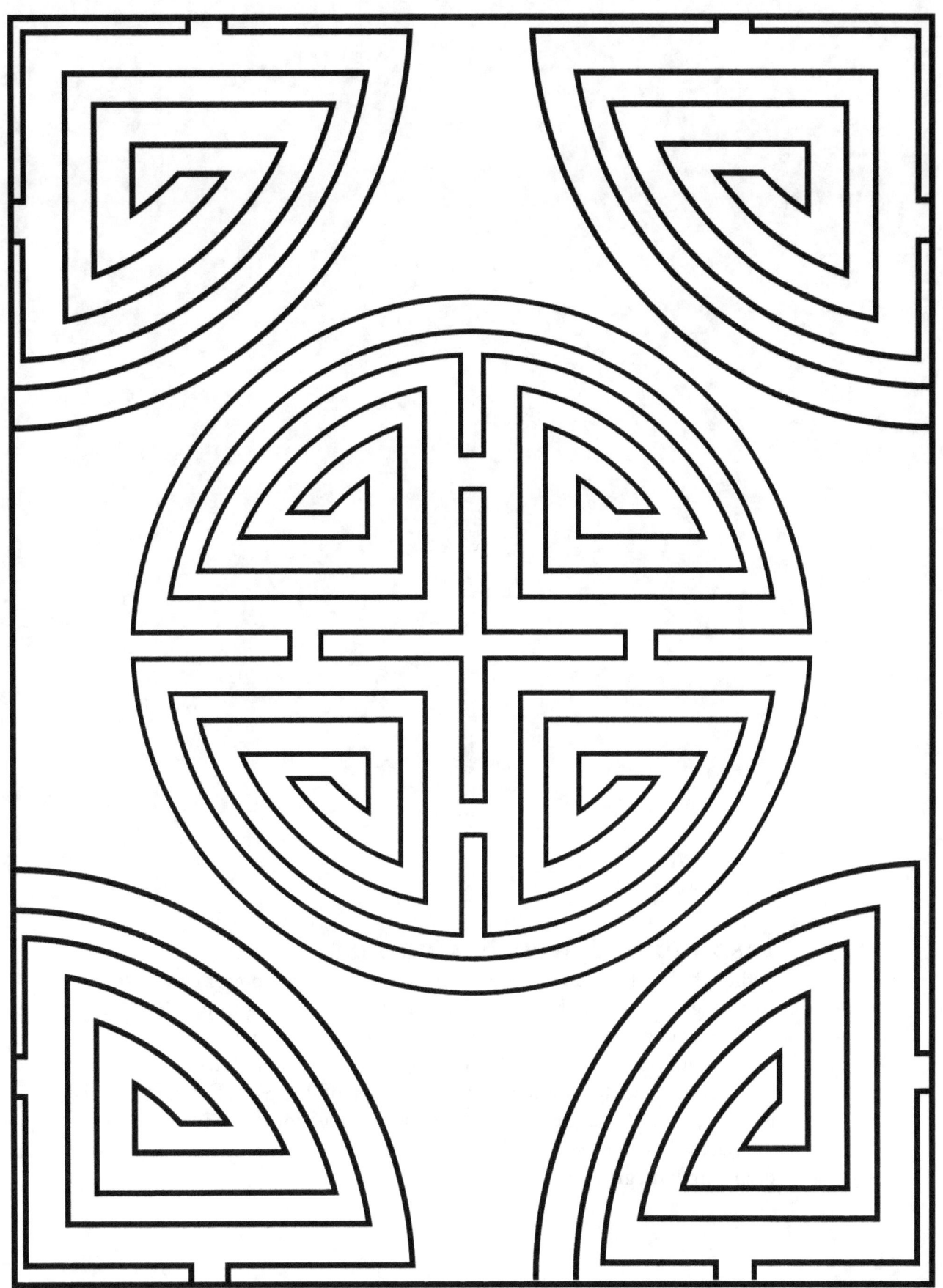

Inspiration: Layers & Contrast

Although this star-shaped design is flat, you can use the power of color to give it a more three dimensional effect by working from brighter colors at the center of the piece to deeper more muted tones on the outer most ring. The contrast in both color and intensity will make the bright center seem to pop off the page. For instance, choose a bright color like yellow or orange for the center to visually draw the eye away from your outer darker tones like a deep burgundy, green or grey.

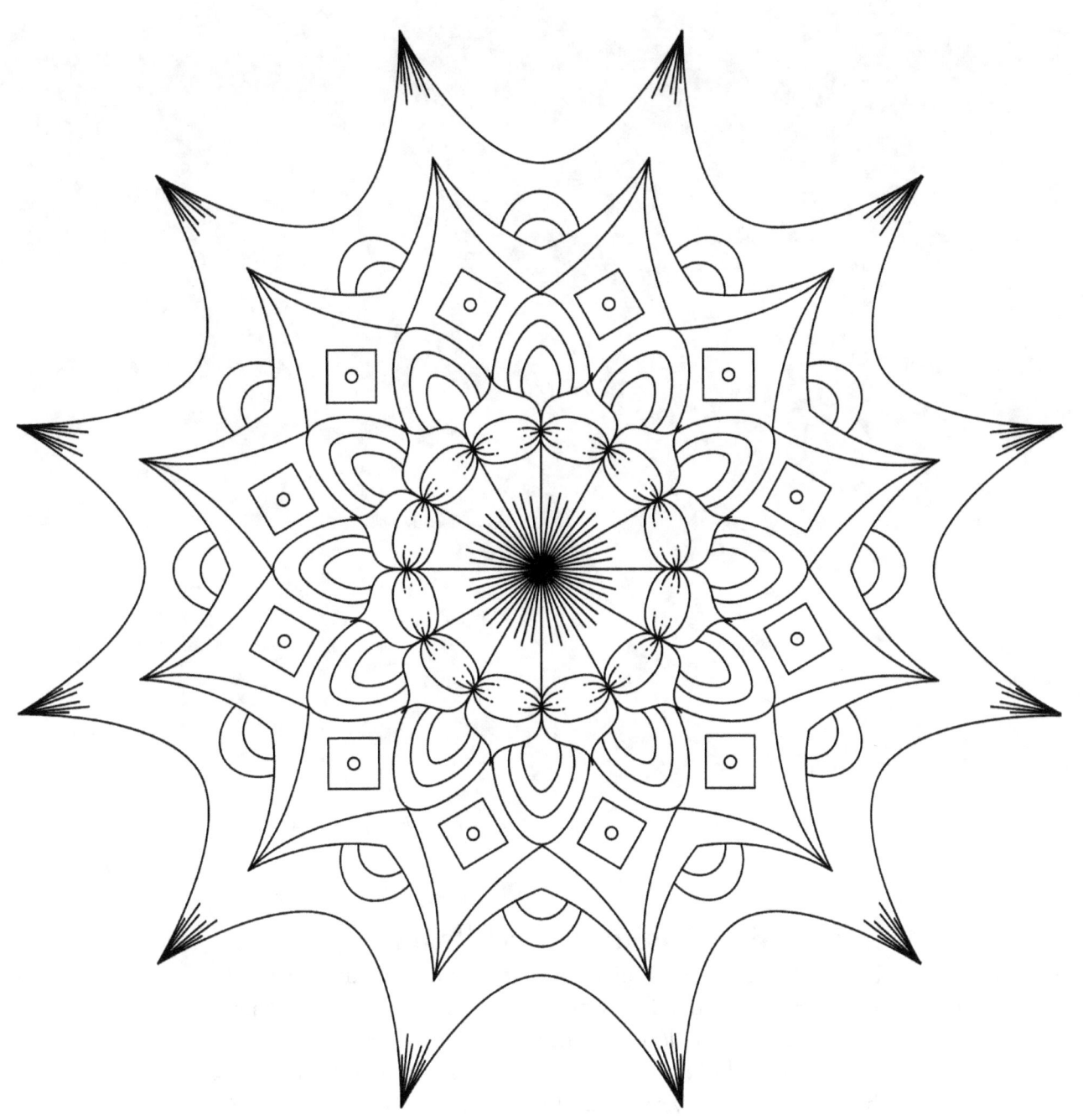

Inspiration: Balance and Peace

The act of drawing a circular design can have a meditative effect
on the craftsperson. Often when I'm feeling the most unbalanced,
I draw symmetrical designs with lots of loosely curving flowing
lines. When coloring this style of mandala, you might select colors
that make you happy and peaceful. Imagine the colors of a sunrise
or sunset, the hues of a moutain or forest, or simply be inspired by
your favorite place.

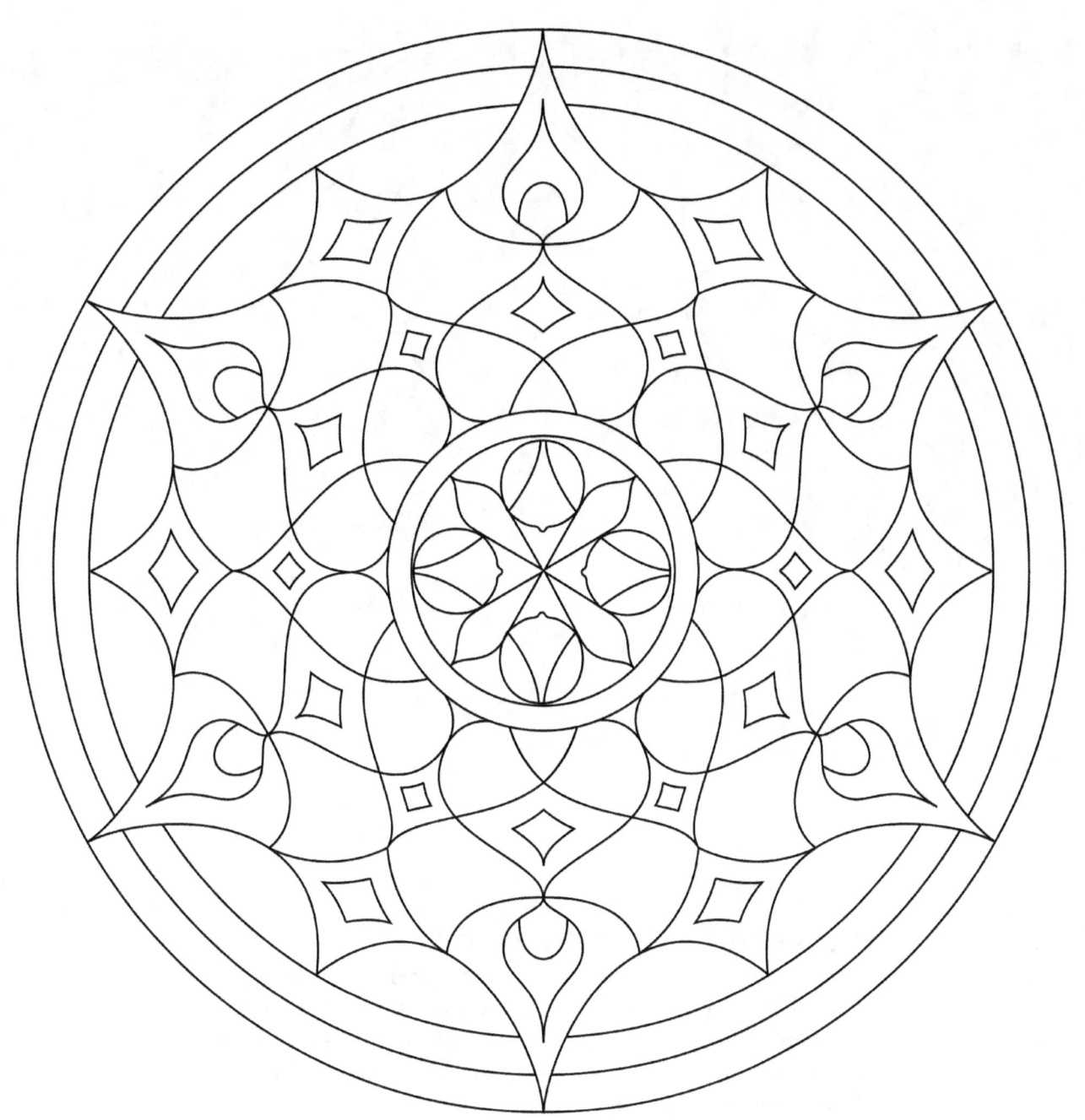

Inspiration: Make it Bigger

When you run accross a mandala in a large open space, why not add some additional rows of design to expand the design outward to the edge of the page. Another approach is to fill the empty or negative space with doodles to fill up your page. Nervous? Use a fine point pencil to draw out your design and then when you like the way it looks, go over in pen and erase the pencil lines. Then color away!

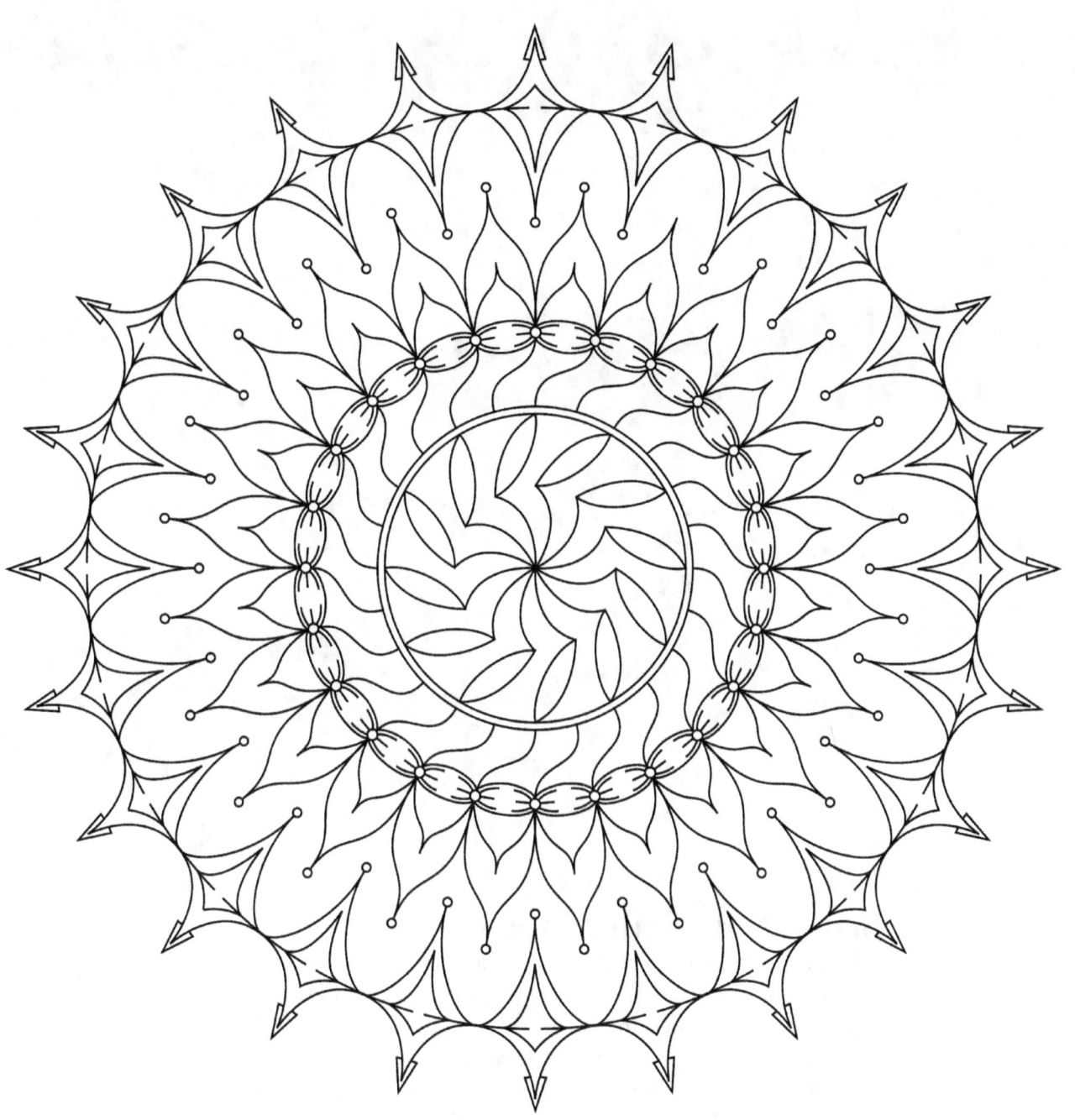

Inspiration: Stained Glass

Bright and brilliant color has been used to create stained glass windows for centuries. The process of making stained glass involves creating a design in lead strips that enclose strategically designed pieces of glass. The framework of lead is soldered together to hold everything in place. When light shines through the brilliant colors, they create an otherworldly effect. Try filling in the areas outside the frame with black to enhance the stained glass effect of this design.

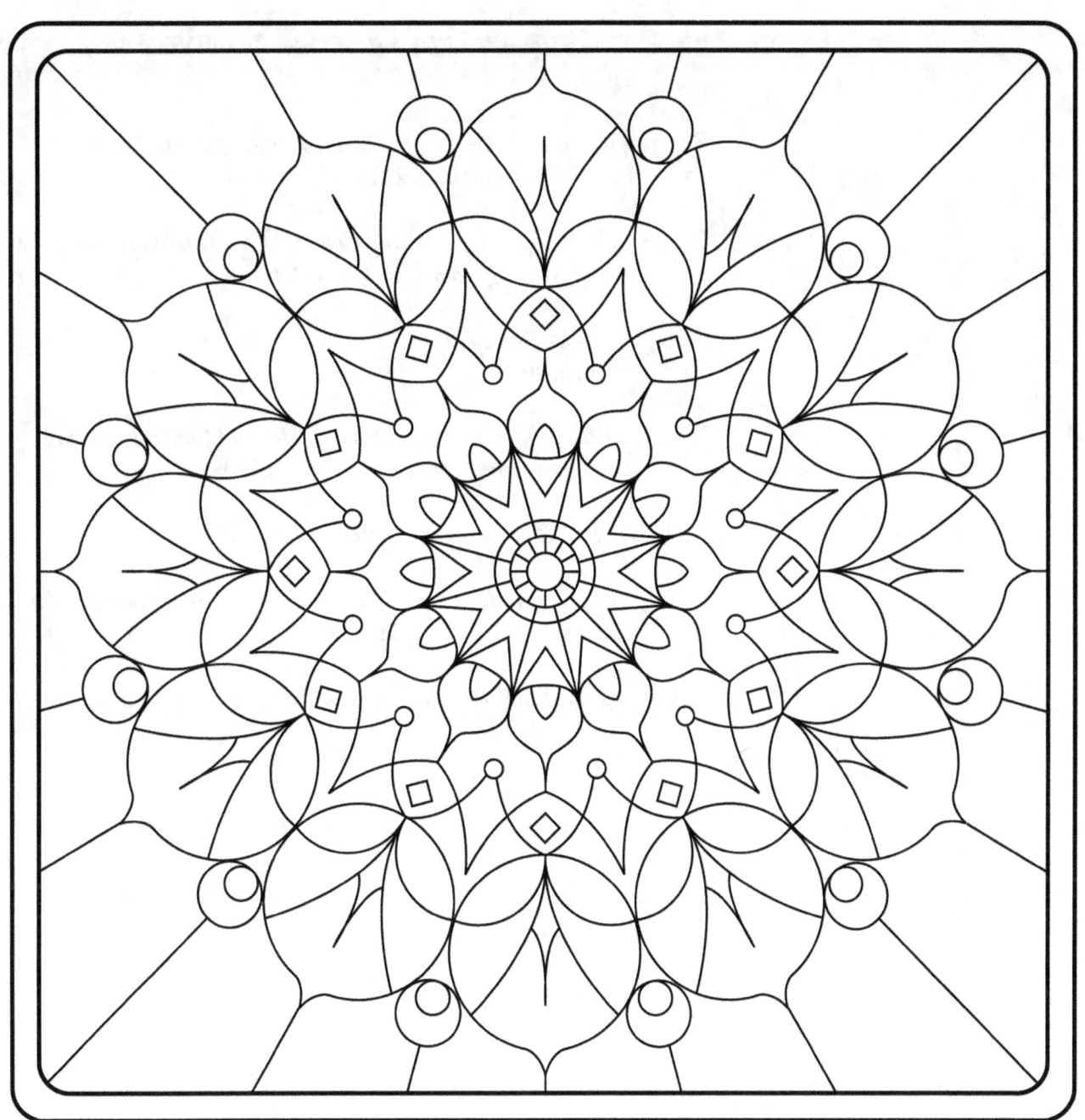

Reading List

Aimone, Steven. *Design! A Lively Guide to Design Basics for Artists & Craftspeople.* Lark Books, 2004.

Birren, Faber. *Itten: The Elements of Color.* John Wiley & Sons, 1970.

Eckstut, Joann and Arielle. *The Secret Language of Color.* Workman Publishing Co., 2013.

Edwards, Betty. *The Art of Using Color: A Course in Mastering the Art of Mixing Colors.* Putnam, 2004.

Finlay, Victoria. *The Brilliant History of Color in Art.* Getty Publications, 2014.

Leland, Nita. *Exploring Color: How to Use and Control Color in Your Painting.* North Light Books, 1998.

Mollica, Patti. *Color Theory.* Walter Foster, 2013.

Quiller, Stephen. *Color Choices: Making Color Sense Out of Color Theory.* Watson-Guptill, 1989.

Seivewright, Simon. *Research and Design.* Ava Publishing, 2007.

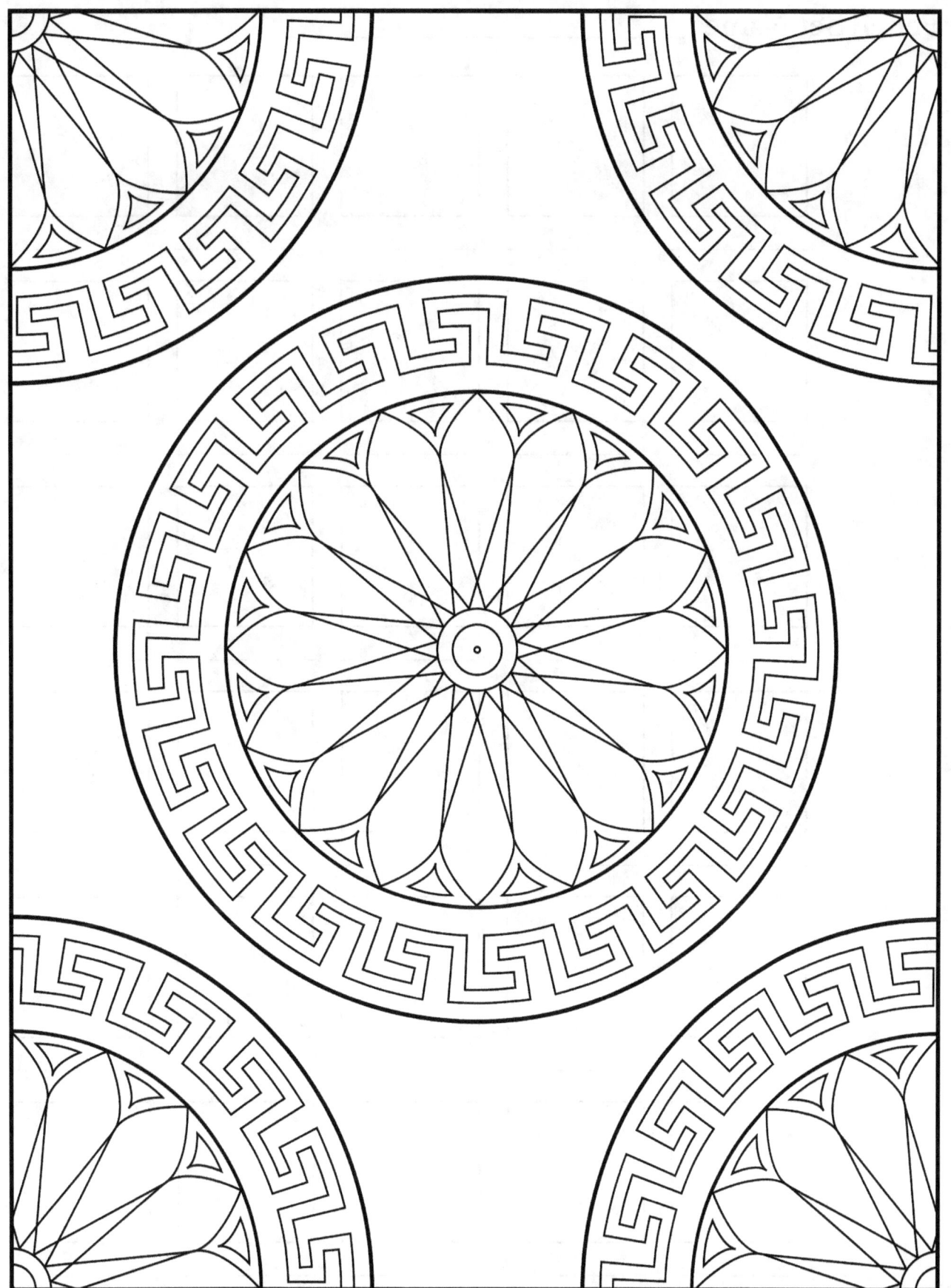

Pencil Set Name _____

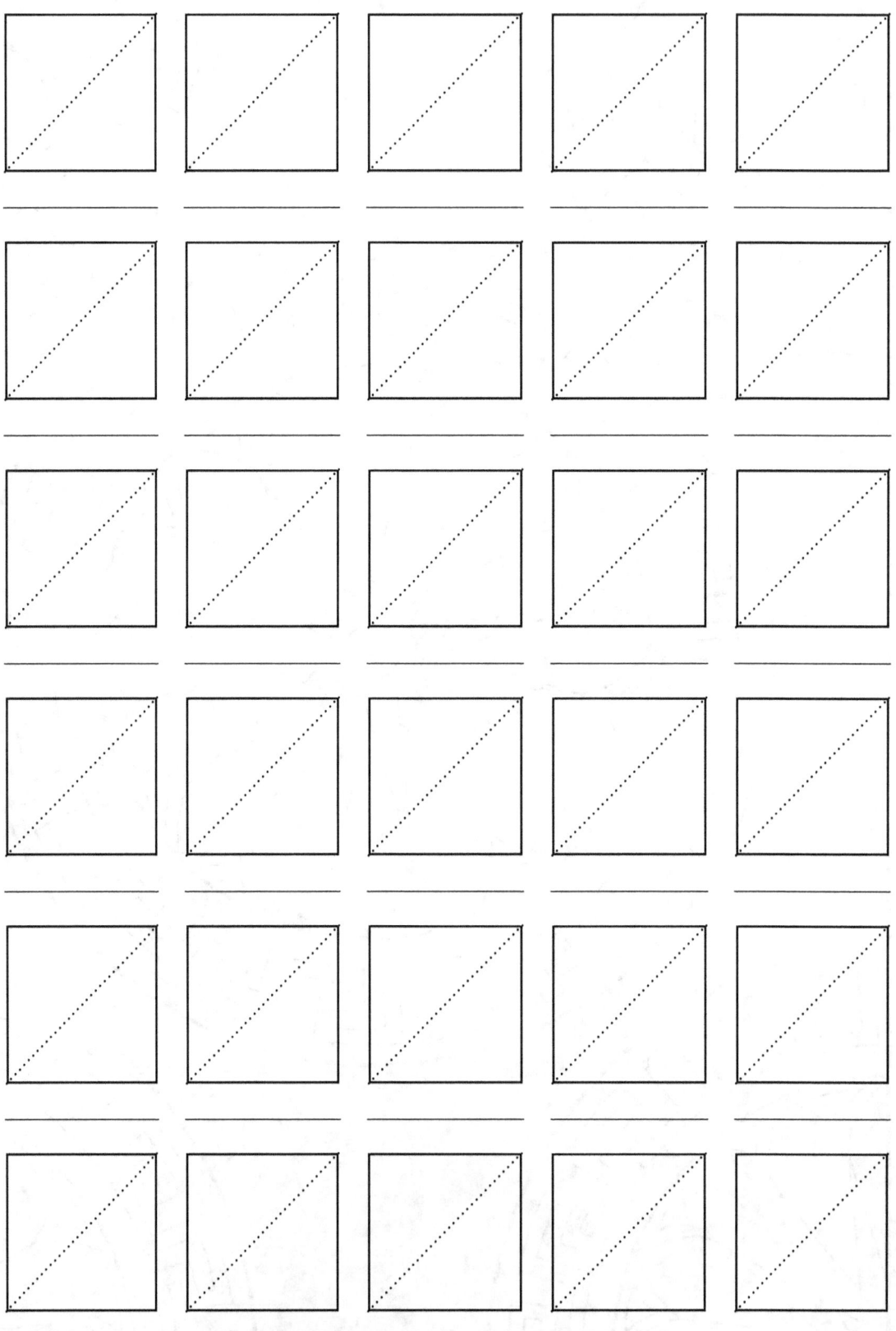

Pencil Set Name _____

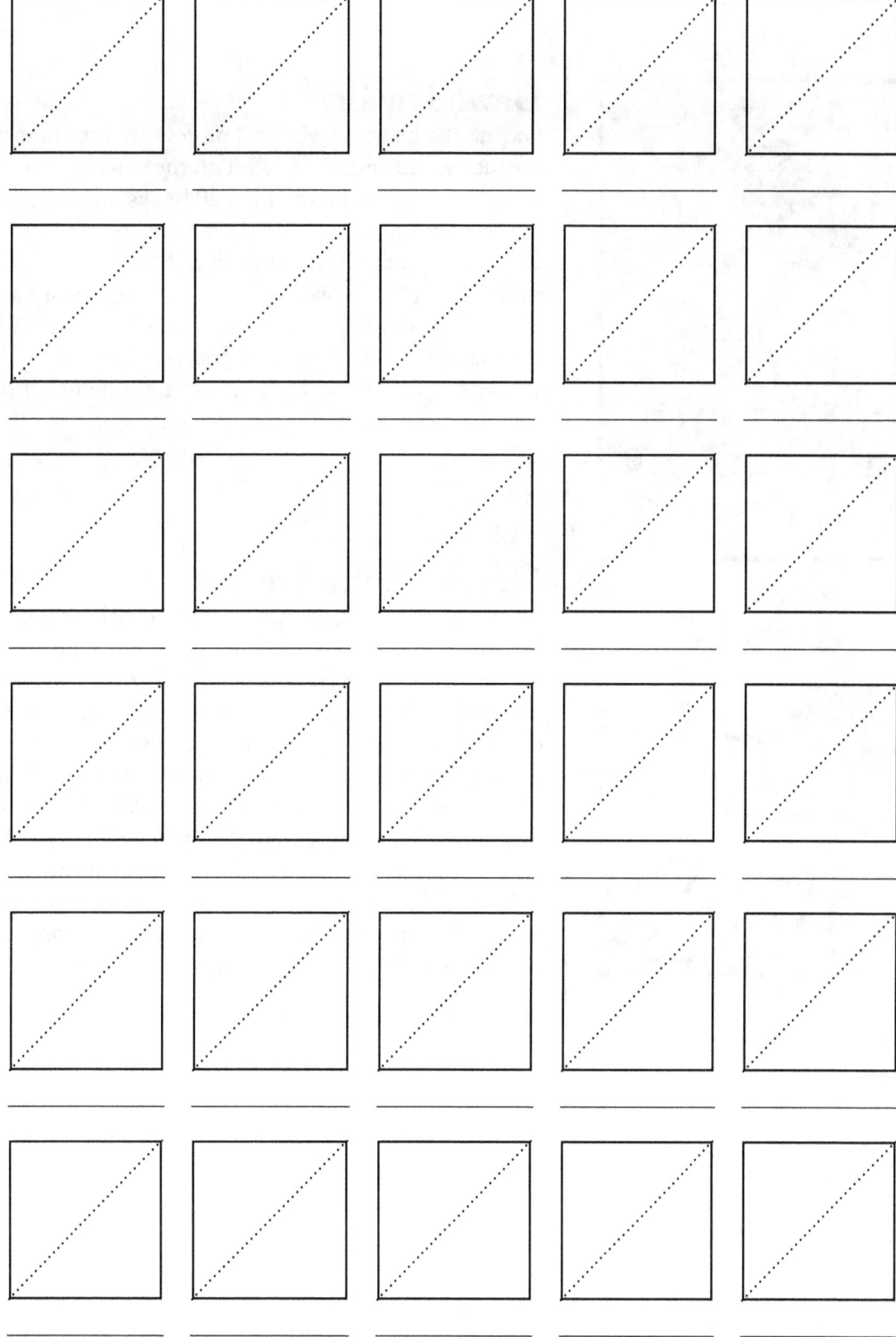

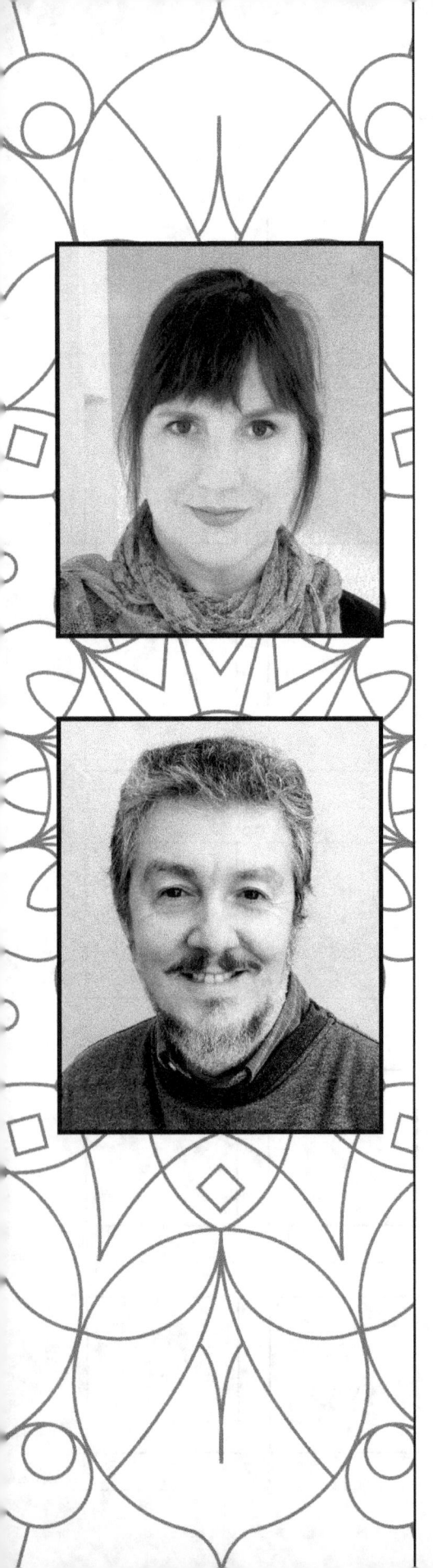

About the Authors

Dawn Devine

Davina aka Dawn Devine is a professional costume designer, instructor, and author focussed on the world of dance costuming. She's published more than 20 books including her best selling "Embellished Bras" and the seminal textile history book "The Cloth of Egypt: All About Assiut." She has travelled near and wide sharing her knowledge of costuming, history, and dance in classes, lectures, and workshops. Dawn has an active blog where she shares her costuming and design projects. Visit her website for a more detailed bio and to find out more about her publications. www.davina.us

George Goncalves

The art in this book, George's second collaboration with Ibexa Press, represents a real collaborative effort, allowing for both author and artist to produce images that are a true reflection of a symbiotic experience. The give and take involved in the creation of each image resulted in a curated collection of coloring book images that is more targeted than any one isolated effort could be. When not exploring the world of mandalas George's work draws on many influences that have fascinated him since childhood: Ligne Claire, comic book art, the dynamic illustration style of the 50's and 60's, to name a few. The magical world of the performing arts has also long been a source of inspiration, often explored through a variety of computer arts techniques.

Other Books by the Authors

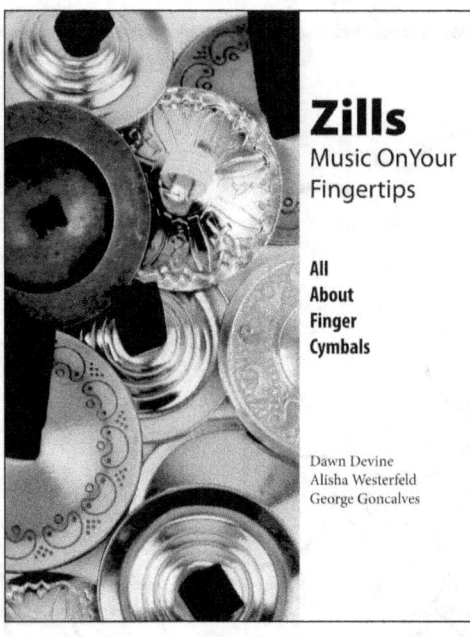

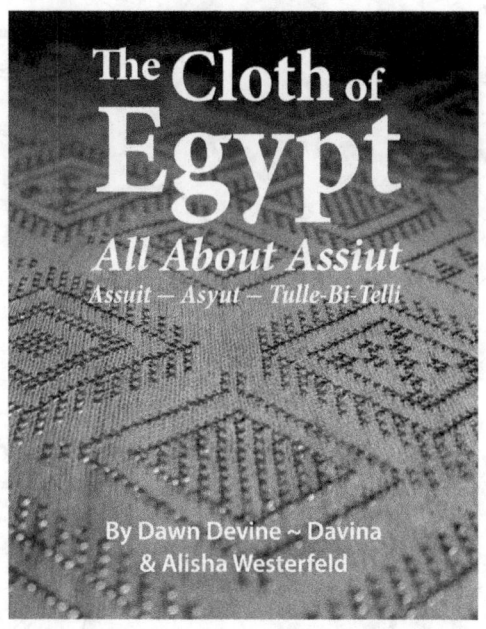

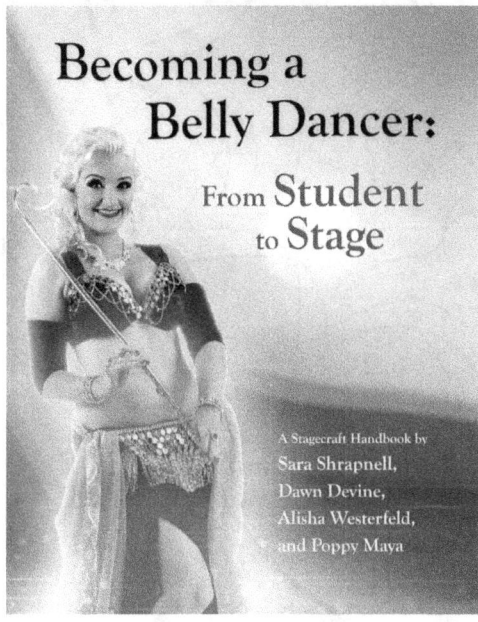

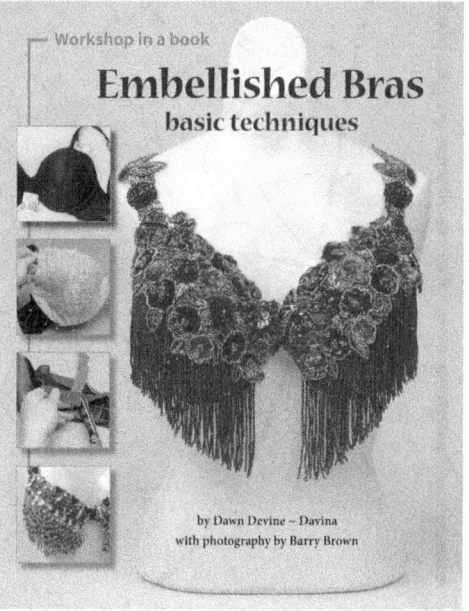

For more information about Dawn Devine aka Davina
and her complete collection of books and digital
publications and social media connections,
visit her website:

www.davina.us

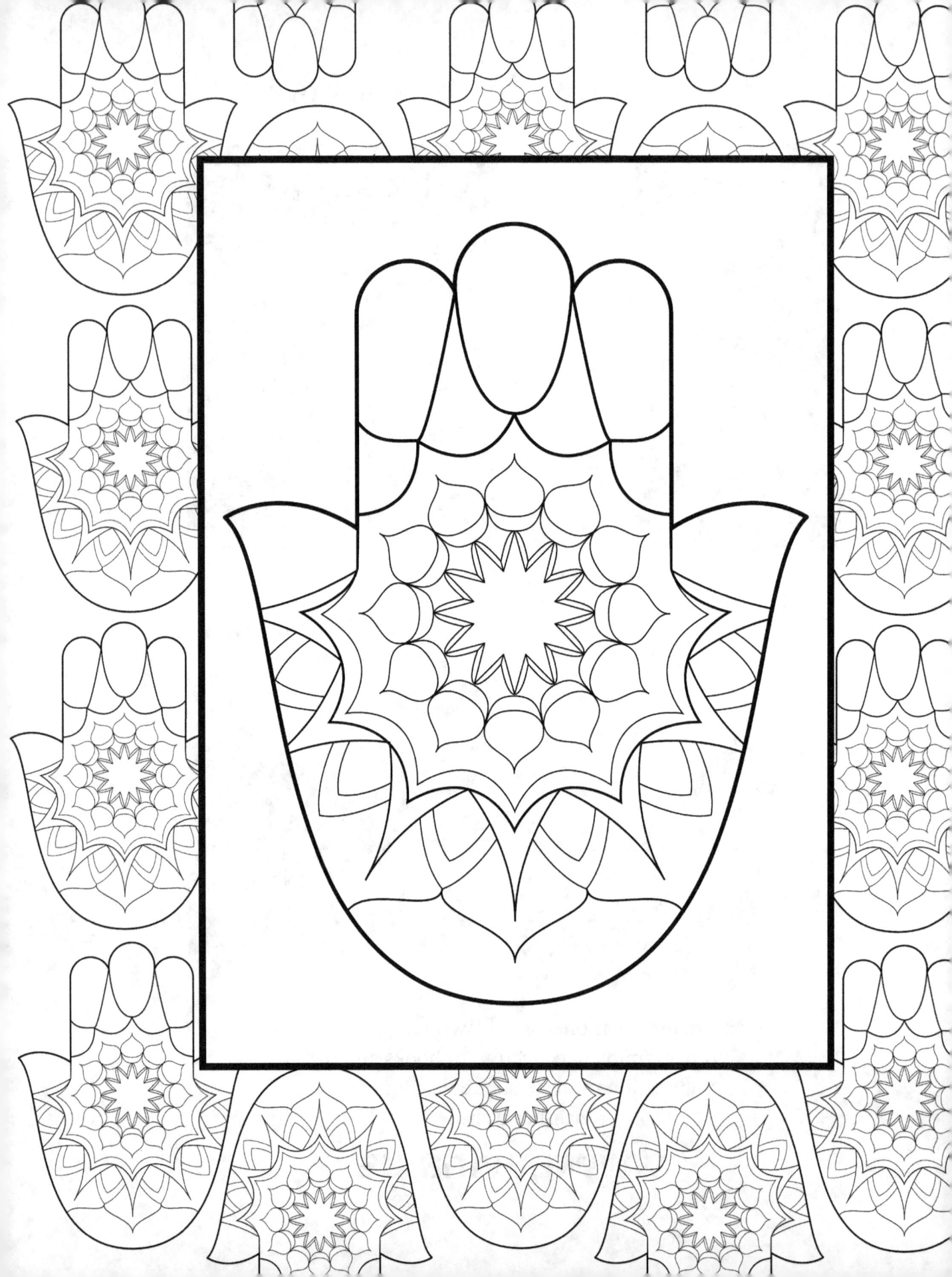